World Wisdom
The Library of Perennial Philosophy

The Library of Perennial Philosophy is dedicated to the exposition of the timeless Truth underlying the diverse religions. This Truth, often referred to as the *Sophia Perennis*—or Perennial Wisdom—finds its expression in the revealed Scriptures as well as the writings of the great sages and the artistic creations of the traditional worlds.

A Treasury of Sufi Wisdom appears as one of our selections in the Treasures of the World's Religions series.

Treasures of the World's Religions Series

This series of anthologies presents scriptures and the writings of the great spiritual authorities of the past on fundamental themes. Some titles are devoted to a single spiritual tradition, while others have a unifying topic that touches upon traditions from both the East and West, such as prayer and virtue. Some titles have a companion volume within the Perennial Philosophy series.

About This Book

"This elegant and well-chosen anthology of Sufi texts is not only a delight to read, but provides one of the most accessible and useful general introductions to Sufi metaphysics available in English. The emphasis on the mystical fruitfulness of the Qur'ānic texts is especially welcome."
—**Timothy J. Winter**, Cambridge Muslim College, co-author of *Understanding Islam and the Muslims*

"This work brings together some of the most profound and transformative words of wisdom that unveil the mystical heart of the Islamic faith, referred to as Sufism. Given the media coverage of Islam, it is not surprising that many people, all over the world, are wondering how it is that well over one billion Muslims can believe in and practice the religion of Islam: this book will provide a wonderfully clear and spiritually compelling answer."
—**Reza Shah-Kazemi**, Managing Editor, *Encyclopaedia Islamica*, author of *Paths to Transcendence* and *The Other in the Light of the One*

"Drawing on over one hundred different sources and classical texts, Peter Samsel has assembled a superb collection of Sufi sayings, anecdotes, aphorisms and poems, *ḥadīth* and Qur'ānic citations concerning divine Unity, and the contemplative discipline of invocation of God (*dhikr*) in Sufism. The author's own extremely original and insightful analysis of the doctrine of Unity in Sufism reveals the ecumenism at the heart of exoteric Muslim fideism."
—**Leonard Lewisohn**, University of Exeter, editor of *The Philosophy of Ecstasy*

"This remarkably wide-ranging volume can be read in two very different, yet complementary ways. First of all, Dr. Samsel has provided an inspiring and thought-provoking collection of spiritual wisdom and insights drawn from the Qur'ān, *ḥadīth*, and more than a hundred classical Sufi authors and teachers, together representing all the major genres of Islamic spiritual writing. Readers from every background will discover some familiar voices, such as Rūmī's poetry, alongside equally intriguing passages from figures who are less well known today, together offering a richly elaborate 'bedside' treasury of meditations and guides to spiritual practice. At the same time, for more systematic readers, these beautiful (and bountiful) selected passages are presented here within a carefully elaborated metaphysical and philosophical framework that together may well provide the most intelligible, widely accessible, and persuasively articulated introduction to the classical Islamic theological tradition available today."

—**James W. Morris**, Boston College, author of *The Reflective Heart*

A Treasury of Sufi Wisdom

The Path of Unity

Foreword by

Seyyed Hossein Nasr

Edited by

Peter Samsel

World Wisdom

A Treasury of Sufi Wisdom: The Path of Unity

Most recent printing indicated by last digit below:
10 9 8 7 6 5 4 3 2

Library of Congress Cataloging-in-Publication Data

A treasury of Sufi wisdom : the path of unity / foreword by Seyyed Hossein
Nasr ; edited by Peter Samsel.
pages cm. -- (The library of perennial philosophy)
Includes bibliographical references and index.
ISBN 978-1-936597-46-8 (alk. paper)
1. Sufism. 2. Sufis. I. Nasr, Seyyed Hossein. II. Samsel, Peter.
BP189.T67 2015
297.4--dc23
2015023674

Printed on acid-free paper in the United States of America.

For information address World Wisdom, Inc.
P.O. Box 2682, Bloomington, Indiana 47402-2682
www.worldwisdom.com

For Gail,
beloved companion on the path.

Contents

List of Figures

Foreword

The doctrine of Unity (*tawḥīd*) is the central doctrine of Islam just as the attainment of Unity stands as the ultimate goal of all Islamic practice. This is especially the case in Islamic spirituality and esoterism, which have been crystallized over the centuries largely in Sufism, whose central spiritual method is the *dhikr*—the invocation and remembrance of God. The central testimony (*Shahādah*) of Islam, that "there is no god but God" (*lā ilāha illa 'Llāh*), is the doctrinal foundation of Unity. In turn, the invocation of the *Shahādah*, along with that of the Divine Name that it contains, is the fundamental means of remembering God and attaining Unity. God is One, the only One, and that Reality requires, most immediately, integration on the human plane and ultimately the realization that the One alone *is* and we are not, our selfhood having passed away or become annihilated (*fanā'*), and that finally He is the Self of our selves, that our true self subsists in Him (*baqā'*).

In this exceptionally succinct and lucid work, Peter Samsel deals in six chapters, which follow each other with an inner logic, with the theme of unity from both a doctrinal and a methodological perspective, but always in an essential and principial manner. Following an overview in the opening chapter, he deals in a most wide-ranging manner in the second and third chapters with the doctrine of Unity and in the fourth and fifth chapters with the method to attain unity and with its realization. The final chapter draws all of these aspects of Unity together in an integral vision. So, the work is at once a doctrinal and practical guide to what lies at the heart of Sufism. Needless to say, however, the actual practice of the method requires a qualified guide. No matter how good a written guide may be for climbing high mountain peaks, the actual climbing requires a seasoned guide without whom one could experience an irreparable fall.

One of the outstanding features of this book is that it is replete with quotations from Sufi masters ranging from the earliest period to recent times. One could in fact say that the work is a very well chosen anthology of Sufi aphorisms, sayings, poetry, and teachings containing many pearls of the vast literature of Sufism. The selection of the Sufi quotations reveals the extensive knowledge Peter Samsel has of Sufi literature as well as his mastery of Sufi doctrine and intimate familiarity with Sufi practice.

In a world in which there are so many distorted or truncated expositions of Sufism, it is important to point out the authentic presentation of this book, rooted as it is in the Sufi tradition and the traditional worldview. This work thus serves as a sure guide for the understanding of authentic Sufi doctrine and the principles of the method of reaching the Truth which the doctrine explains and to whose realization it points. Like all authentic Sufi works, it provides a map, often in the words of great masters, of the path to the Truth and instructions concerning how to follow the path. It challenges the reader to ask himself or herself who he or she is, what is the meaning of being human, and where he or she is going and should be going. Its aim is both propaedeutic and therapeutic. Let us hope that it will cause the perceptive reader to realize why we are here and where we should be going in this transient and fleeting life, thus becoming a true seeker. And let us not forget that as Christ said, "Seek and ye shall find."

Seyyed Hossein Nasr
Muharram 1436 AH
October, 2014 AD

Introduction

Sometimes, the simplest of stated truths can carry the most subtle and profound ramifications. Sometimes, the deepest mystery of reality can be signified in a single, effulgent word. For Islam, that Abrahamic monotheism most thoroughly concerned with the singularity and universality of the Divine, that word is "Unity." God is One, or as the concise creedal statement of Islam—the *Shahādah*—expresses it, "There is no god but God" (*lā ilāha illā 'Llāh*). Strictly speaking, this is the first of two *Shahādahs*, respectively addressing metaphysics and prophethood;[1] it is this first *Shahādah*—which has formed the most persistent and widespread motif of Islamic civilization—that is of particular concern in the present anthology. Yet although the *Shahādah* is central to the larger tradition, it has been the particular task of the Sufis—those representatives of the spiritual interiority of the Islamic faith—to draw forth the full meaning and consequences for the human spirit of this foundational understanding.

Sufism is a vast and varied historical and civilizational phenomenon, touching upon poetic expression and sacred art, ethics and virtue, discipleship and spiritual guidance, humble service and spiritual practice, the nourishment of the heart and the illumination of vision. Yet all these many concerns coalesce ultimately to a single concern: that of the return to God. The way of this return is, at root, a matter of the ever-deepening inculcation of the reality of Divine Unity in one's being, as expressed in one's understanding, one's presence and attention, and ultimately one's very existence. This "Path of Unity" is none other than the central course of the entire tradition of Sufism. What does it mean to inculcate the reality of Divine Unity? It means, in essence, to become "one" oneself, for the return to God calls for the whole of oneself. This unification of the human being towards God is closely related to the virtue of sincerity (*ikhlās*), of being both one-minded and whole-hearted.

In this sense, the "Path of Unity" bears a twofold meaning, for it is at once a path toward the One, as well as a path of self-unification, for—to express the matter aphoristically—the Unity of God is only

[1] The second *Shahādah*, addressing prophethood, states that "Muḥammad is the messenger of God" (*Muḥammadun rasūlu 'Llāh*). Chapter VI treats both the first and second *Shahādah* in detail.

to be realized through the unity of the human self. This unification may also be understood in terms of worship (*'ibāda*), as expressed, for instance, in the Qur'ānic assertion "There is no god but I, so worship Me" (21:25). Here, Divine Unity may be said to impel human unification as its necessary consequence. The understanding of human unification towards God in terms of worship recalls once more the *Shahādah*, the creedal statement of unity that, at its most basic level, forms the essence of worship in Islam. That "there is no god but God" may be understood simply and straightforwardly as a claim of absolute monotheism, but the Sufi tradition has further seen this as the quintessential statement of the purest metaphysics, for by extension there are not only no other gods, but more profoundly no independent reality apart from God, who is at once the sole Principle and Ground of existence.

This metaphysical understanding, the doctrine of Unity (*tawḥīd*), represents, at the level of human intellectual conceptualization, an aspect of human unification with respect to God, for to deeply plumb the mysteries of *tawḥīd* is to that extent to become one-minded and to perceive the traces of the Divine Presence in all things. Yet this is only one level, for while many may grasp subtle metaphysics, it is necessary to be not merely one-minded but one-pointed, to concentrate one's attention upon God as well as to sustain that concentration in time. Heedlessness of the Divine Reality is the very failure of both sincerity and worship. It is here that the spiritual practice of the remembrance of God (*dhikr*)—either through the invocatory repetition of the Divine Name or the *Shahādah* itself—may be seen as a further concomitant of the *Shahādah*.

In the perfection of this remembrance there is the forgetfulness of everything apart from God—including oneself—such that, in one's awareness, there is only God. This lived experience is described in Sufism as the "passing away" or "annihilation" (*fanā'*) of the self and the "subsistence" (*baqā'*) of God. Such an experience is recognized by the Sufi tradition as the subjective unveiling of what is, metaphysically, the actual and objective state of affairs, not only for oneself, but for all created existence. As the Qur'ān states, "Everything upon the earth is undergoing annihilation, but there subsists the Face of your Lord, Possessor of Majesty and Generous Giving" (55:26-27). The Reality of the Divine necessarily implies the contingency of creation, for all is sustained by God at every instant. This realization of the Divine subsistence is, in a sense, at once the ultimate ramification and validation of the truth of the *Shahādah*.

To summarize then, what we have termed the Path of Unity—this golden thread of return that runs through the Sufi tradition—is comprised of four broad stages: the affirmation of Unity, as witnessed in the testimony of the *Shahādah*; the discernment of Unity, as elaborated in the metaphysics of *tawḥīd*; the concentration upon Unity, enabled through the invocatory practice of *dhikr*, and finally, the realization of Unity, as particularly evinced in the experience of *fanā'* and *baqā'*.

As central as these stages are to the tradition of Sufism, their collective coherence and significance is not necessarily easy to discern for those unfamiliar with Sufi teachings. Further, the testimonies and teachings that address these stages of return are scattered throughout the tradition. Our aim in the present anthology has been to gather and organize these many voices of the Sufi tradition that elucidate this Path of Unity. Sufi teaching has historically encompassed a considerable range of expression, including aphorisms, poetry, table talks, letters of guidance, lives of saints, texts of spiritual instruction, and treatises of metaphysical doctrine. The accessibility of such teaching has varied accordingly, with such expressions as Sufi poetry having enjoyed a widespread appeal, while others, such as difficult philosophic works, have necessarily found a more limited and elite audience.

While keeping to shorter, more accessible writings, we have endeavored to present a variety of these expressive styles, including brief aphorisms, spiritual poetry, and short texts and excerpts of spiritual instruction or doctrinal elucidation. We have also included relevant passages from the Qur'ān and sayings of Muḥammad (*ḥadīth*), as well as the handful of extra-Qur'ānic sayings from Muḥammad that are nevertheless held to be of Divine origin (*ḥadīth qudsī*). These foundational sources of the Islamic tradition are not uncommonly the direct inspirations for Sufi reflection and exposition, which in many instances cannot be properly or fully situated without reference to them.[2]

There is another reason for the inclusion of these foundational Islamic sources in the present work. Although an earlier strain of Orientalist scholarship considered Sufism to have its origins outside of the Islamic tradition, more recent scholarship, beginning with that of the French Catholic Islamicist Louis Massignon more than ninety years ago, has definitively established that Sufism is inherent

[2] All Qur'ānic passages are followed with colon-separated chapter and verse number referencing, as in the prior quoted passages.

to Islam, grounded both upon the text of the Qur'ān and example of Muḥammad. Despite both this and its historically central role within the Islamic tradition, Sufism has been more recently contested within the Islamic world both by modernists and fundamentalists, who—for very different reasons—have challenged its Islamic legitimacy.

Such an attempt to sunder Sufism from its Islamic context would at once deny Sufism its proper foundation as well as strip Islam of its higher spiritual, artistic, and intellectual possibilities. The consequence of such a sundering would be a twofold poverty, at once for Sufism as well as for the larger tradition. The incorporation of foundational Islamic sources in direct relation to Sufi writings in the present anthology serves not only to illuminate those same writings, but also to demonstrate the close connection between the two, and thereby to validate, in some measure, the legitimacy of Sufism within the Islamic tradition.

In a larger sense, however, the clearest demonstration of this legitimacy in the context of the guiding theme of the present work is that this central Path of Unity of the Sufi tradition is, at root, a working out of the ramifications of that most foundational of Islamic understandings, that "There is no god but God." Everything follows from this, just as, in a sense, everything returns to it as well. Yet, while there is no saying more decisive to or representative of the Islamic tradition than this, it is nevertheless not limitatively Islamic at all, but rather, as previously noted, purely metaphysical, such that sages quite apart from the Islamic tradition, such as Plotinus, Meister Eckhart, Śaṅkarācārya, or Chuang Tzu, could—with suitable reformulation to their respective traditions—readily lend it credence. Within an Islamic perspective, this should be thoroughly unsurprising, for one of the insistent points of the Qur'ānic discourse is precisely that its core message is at once universal and unoriginal to the Islamic tradition.

To address the sources of the present anthology in somewhat greater detail, we have included contributions from nearly a hundred Sufi figures, from the famous to the more obscure, ranging across the history and breadth of Islamic civilization, including nearly all of those most significant to the Sufi tradition—devoted souls such as Rābi'a al-'Adawīya and Yūnus Emre, poetic sages such as Jalāl ad-Dīn Rūmī and Fakhr ad-Dīn 'Irāqī, profound metaphysicians such as Muḥyī ad-Dīn Ibn al-'Arabī and Abū'l-Qāsim al-Junayd, daring figures such as Bāyazīd al-Bisṭāmī and Ḥusayn Ibn Manṣūr al-Ḥallāj, theologians and philosophers such as Abū Ḥāmid al-Ghazālī and Ṣadr ad-Dīn Qūnawī, wise counselors such as 'Abd al-Qādir al-Jīlānī and Abū Sa'īd

Ibn Abī'l-Khayr, spiritual guides such as Ibn 'Aṭā' Allāh al-Iskandarī and Sharaf ad-Dīn Manīrī, and great saints such as Abū Madyan and Abū'l-Ḥasan ash-Shādhilī.

Further, we have included contributions from a number of the most significant companions of Muḥammad, including Abū Bakr aṣ-Ṣiddīq, 'Umar ibn al-Khattāb and, perhaps most significantly, 'Alī ibn Abī Ṭālib, whose metaphysical mastery and spiritual insight were to have a profound influence upon the entire subsequent tradition of Sufism.

We have structured the present anthology in four principal sections, addressing each of the four broad stages of the Path of Unity in turn. Within each of these sections, we have endeavored to draw out and thematically organize the various contributing passages into distinct subcategories. Further, we have attempted, at the beginning of each section, to elucidate the relational structure of the relevant subcategories in figural form. These diagrammatic figures collectively provide a capsule summary of the entire Path of Unity in all of its coherence and comprehensiveness and should prove valuable in providing an overview for the reader. We have further provided an introduction for each section, summarizing the stage in question and elucidating the details of the related diagrammatic figure. Finally, we include an initial, brief overview section and accompanying figure, demonstrating the broad line of connection between these four stages.

Following these four sections, we have further included a concluding essay, "The *Shahādah* and the Path of Unity," that serves as a complement to the anthological offerings of the previous sections, treating the Path of Unity in relation to the *Shahādah* in a systematic and extended matter not possible in the context of the shorter passages of the anthology proper.

Peter Samsel

I. The Path of Unity: The Twofold Movement of the Stages of Return

In the Context of *Tawḥīd*	Misattribution of the Real	Recognition of the Real
Human Orientation (unbelief / faith)	*kufr* (concealing God) ←	→ *īmān* (affirming God)
Divine Indication (hidden / revealed)	*ḥijāb* (Divine veil) ←	→ *wajh* (Divine Face)
Experienced Identity (subject / Subject)	*nafs* (soul) ←	→ *al-Ḥaqq* (Divine Reality)

Realization of *Tawḥīd*	Negation of the unreal	Affirmation of the Real
Affirmation of Unity (*Shahādah*)	*nafy* (negation): *lā ilāha* ("no god") →	*ithbāt* (affirmation): *illā Allāh* ("but God")
Discernment of Unity (*tawḥīd*)	denial of apparent multiplicity →	affirmation of actual Unity
Concentration upon Unity (*dhikr*)	forgetfulness of the world →	remembrance of God
Realization of Unity (*fanā' / baqā'*)	annihilation from self →	subsistence of God

I. The Path of Unity: The Stages of Return

If the predominating theme of the Islamic tradition is that of Divine Unity and the predominating concern of Sufism is the recovery of that unity, the context in which both are situated is nevertheless that of the multiplicity of the created order. The assertion of the tradition—in conjunction with other sacred traditions—is that this multiplicity is relatively unreal, only apparently real, or a misattribution of an underlying Reality.

This misattribution appears in three principal domains: In the first, that of human orientation, it manifests as unbelief, what the tradition terms *kufr*, or concealing God. In the second, that of what may be termed the Divine indication, it manifests as the hiddenness of God, the Divine veil or *ḥijāb*—related to what Hindu metaphysics terms *māyā*—by which multiplicity appears manifest. In the third, that of experienced identity, it manifests as the human soul itself or *nafs*, which may be understood as the immediate, subjective aspect of the Divine hiddenness in the context of an apparent multiplicity.

The coordinate recognition of the Real applies similarly to these same three domains: In that of human orientation, unbelief is corrected by faith or affirming God, what the tradition terms *īmān*. In that of the Divine indication, the Divine veil occludes the Divine Face or *wajh*, which stands behind it but also shines through it—what is veil from one perspective is revealed as theophany from another, just as created multiplicity is seen as nothing but a manifestation of Divine Unity. In that of experienced identity, the soul or human subject is none other than a seat of the Divine Reality, or *al-Ḥaqq*—"the throne of the All-Merciful," as the tradition expresses it—which is the Divine Face in the context of immediate subjectivity.

In all three domains, the distinction between an apparent multiplicity and an actual, underlying Unity results in two broad possibilities: either misattribution of the Real—in fact, affirmation of the relatively unreal—or, alternatively, recognition of the Real. This twofold distinction, between the unreal and the Real, in turn necessitates a twofold movement of return to the Divine Reality on the part of man, which plays out respectively in each of the four stages of the Path of Unity.

At the stage of the creedal affirmation of Unity, associated with the *Shahādah*, the negation of the unreal is the first half of the statement of Unity, termed the *nafy* (negation), which states *lā ilāha* ("no god"), denying any ultimate reality apart from God. The affirmation of the Real follows as the second half of the statement, termed the *ithbāt* (affirmation), which states *illā 'Llāh* ("but God"), affirming the sole reality of God. At the stage of the metaphysical discernment of Unity, associated with the doctrine of *tawḥīd*, the negation of the unreal is the denial of apparent multiplicity, while the affirmation of the Real follows as the affirmation of actual Unity. At the stage of concentration upon Unity, associated with the invocatory practice of *dhikr*, the negation of the unreal is the forgetfulness of the world, while the affirmation of the Real follows as the remembrance of God. Finally, at the stage of the realization of Unity, associated with the spiritual stations of *fanā'* and *baqā'*, the negation of the unreal is the annihilation of the self, while the affirmation of the Real follows as the subsistence of God.

Yet all of these movements and stages are only ever in the context of an underlying and overarching Divine Unity, apart from which they have neither meaning nor reality. Only Divine Unity *is*. This is the entire point of the path just described. To give two pointed examples, only God may truly witness to the *Shahādah*—as many Sufis have wryly observed—just as only God may experience the station of Divine subsistence, or *baqā'*. Yet, in a way, multiplicity has its rights as well, for God has in fact created the creation. Creation, in its own paradoxical, highly contingent way, also *is*. A "bare" unity is necessarily simple, but such could never be the ontological seed of all things. Rather, what we face is a "unity in multiplicity" and a "multiplicity in unity," what might be termed with some caution a "manifold unity." It is here, in the midst of this paradoxical condition, that the Sufis have striven—and invite us to strive—upon a path of return to that which always is, to recover what we have always been and yet must become.

II. Affirmation of Unity: The Manifold Aspects of the *Shahādah*

Objective Tawḥīd: No existence but God

	The Shahādah and Divine Reality		
Doctrine	The Statement of the *Shahādah* *creedal certitude* →	The *Shahādah* and *Tawḥīd* *description of the Real*	*Metaphysics*
	The Shahādah and the Life of Faith		
Devotion	The *Shahādah* and Sincerity *singleness of heart* →	The *Shahādah* and Salvation *returning to the Real*	*Deliverance*
	The Spiritual Practice of the Shahādah		
Discipline	The Remembrance of the *Shahādah* *singleness of attention* →	The *Shahādah* and *Fanā'-Baqā'* *realization of the Real*	*Recognition*

Subjective Tawḥīd: No self but God

II. Affirmation of Unity: The Testimony of the *Shahādah*

Overview: The *Shahādah*

On the level of simple belief, the *Shahādah* is, first and foremost a testification of creedal fidelity. It is, in fact, the very entry into faith. Yet it is also a forthright statement of intellectual certitude and as such encompasses at once the domains of both faith and knowledge. Curiously, this double application is reflected in the very meaning of the word *shahādah*, which at once means "to testify" or "to bear witness," but also refers to that which is visible, witnessed, or perceived. Knowledge is a kind of "intellectual perception," and indeed the *Shahādah* may be understood in terms of it being an essential summary of this intellectual perception of Unity, a perception that has been perfectly self-evident to the tradition of Sufism, the broader Islamic intellectual tradition, and indeed to most of the world's sacred traditions.

One may say "There is no god but God" (*lā ilāha illā 'Llāh*) as a statement and act of faith, indeed as a ritual act, but from the perspective of knowledge, one may perfectly well rephrase this as "There is no reality but the Real," where "reality" is understood as that which is absolute, all-encompassing, independent, non-contingent, and unique. It is here that creedal faith passes over into metaphysical description, that fidelity passes over into knowledge, and that the bare words of the formula of the *Shahādah* pass over, as in the grasping of the truth of a mathematical proof, into a state of self-evident certainty.

The *Shahādah* further opens to the virtue of sincerity, for the Unity of God necessitates the unification of one's heart, while the totality of God requires the totality of oneself in response. In this sense, the doctrine of *tawḥīd*, in its metaphysical consequences, directly informs the life of faith. This human response, of sincerity and singleness of heart, calls forth a Divine reply, an opening of return to the Real, to salvation and felicity through the Divine Mercy. In this regard, the Prophetic promise linking the *Shahādah*, the virtue of sincerity, and the gift of Paradise appears with particular emphasis and frequency.

The *Shahādah* is not only a creedal faith and metaphysical doctrine, but also a spiritual means in itself through its incorporation into the practice of the invocatory remembrance of God, or *dhikr*, in which it is frequently used as a formula of recitation, second only to the Divine Name itself. In this way, the *Shahādah* not only opens to singleness of mind through metaphysical certitude and singleness of heart through sincerity of faith, but also to singleness of attention and presence through the discipline of spiritual practice. Finally, the *Shahādah* may be directly experienced as a spiritual condition, in the "annihilation" of *fanā'* and "subsistence" of *baqā'*, when all is revealed as "there is only God."

The Statement of the *Shahādah*

Foundational Sources

Your God is One God; there is no god but He, the All-merciful, the All-compassionate.

– Qur'ān 2:163

God there is no god but He, the Living, the Everlasting.

– Qur'ān 2:255

There is no god but He, the August, the Wise.

– Qur'ān 3:6

Know that it [the Qur'ān] has been sent down with the knowledge of God, and that there is no god but He.

– Qur'ān 11:14

There is no god but He, the Lord of the noble Throne.

– Qur'ān 23:116

So know that there is no god but God, and ask forgiveness of your sin, and for the believers, men and women.

– Qur'ān 47:19

Sufi Poetry

Sweep all away with the broom of "No"! Every king or prince has a herald for every ceremony. The herald which sweeps aside both worlds from before the face of the Courtiers and Kings of Holiness is the phrase:

THERE IS NO GOD BUT GOD

Everything keeps you distant from your quest,
whether words of blasphemy or of belief.
Everything holds you back from the Friend,
whether images of beauty or of beast.
You'll clean no thorn and thistle from this path,
unless the creedal NO serves as your herald.
When NO casts you from fame into confusion,
then follow Godhead's light through BUT to GOD.
– Jalāl ad-Dīn Rūmī [LEW/SS12]

What a banner, what a standard:
There is no god but God!
Planted on the pinnacle of pre-existence:
There is no god but God!
How the King, like Moses, raises dust
from the sea of being and the void!
There is no god but God!
The quality of purity's
modeled on his humility
displayed in God's presence in pre-eternity:
There is no god but God!
One wrong from him bests a billion rights
What wondrous, pleasant tyranny!
There is no god but God!
Every spot where he cast his glance
a million Eden-gardens grow.
There is no god but God!
One fine day from sorrow's sea
I'll reach the shore
cast up by waves of grace and bounty.
There is no god but God!
Any one you see sorrow's grip
has caught no scent
of spirit from my King.
There is no god but God!
All eyes that refuse collyrium
from the King of Tabriz,
what wondrous loss and lamentation!
There is no god but God!
My heart and soul surge with the shout:
"*Are you not?*"

The King hears a thousand voices:
Yes! There is no god but God!
The paradise of grace
the greatness of the prince
Shams ad-Din
What a wondrous cure of suffering:
There is no god but God!
My heart circles
like an intimate
around Tabriz—The *sanctum sanctorum* of
There is no god but God!
How pleasant would it be for me to ask:
Who is it at the door?
and hear him say:
It's me.
There is no god but God!

– Jalāl ad-Dīn Rūmī [LEW/SS7-8]

Sufi Instruction

The phrase *lā ilāha illā 'Llāh* is a sign of knowledge and an affirmation of Unity with the tongue of praise, testifying to the glorious King. When the servant says *lā ilāha illā 'Llāh*, it means that there is no deity who has blessings, favor, power, permanence, majesty, splendor, might, praise, displeasure, and contentment except God, Who is Lord of the Worlds, Creator of the first ones and the last, and Judge of the Day of Judgment.

– Ibn 'Aṭā' Allāh al-Iskandarī [DAN/KS156]

Know that God Almighty has created, in the world of form and image, a form for all that He has brought forth in the world of meaning. . . . The form for the effulgence of the Light of Unity is the affirmation of unity: "There is no god other than God." The profound cause for the sending of the Prophets was the sowing of the seed of that affirmation in the soil of hearts: "This world is a tillage for the hereafter" (*ḥadīth*). Hence it was that the Prophet said: "I have been commanded to fight men until they say: 'There is no god but God.'" What is meant by this if not the scattering of the seed of Unity on the soil of men's hearts? *Hast thou not seen how God has struck a similitude? A good word is as a good tree—its roots are firm, and its branches are in heaven; it gives its fruit every season by the leave of its Lord. Thus God strikes similitudes for men, that haply they may remember*(14:24-25).

– Najm ad-Dīn Rāzī [ALG/GB92-93]

The *Shahādah* and *Tawḥīd*

Foundational Sources

He is God;
there is no god but He.
He is the knower of the Unseen and the Visible;
He is the All-merciful, the All-compassionate.

He is God;
there is no god but He.
He is the King, the All-holy, the All-peaceable,
the All-faithful, the All-preserver,
the All-mighty, the All-compeller, the All-sublime.
Glory be to God, above that they associate!

He is God,
the Creator, the Maker, the Shaper.
To Him belong the Names Most Beautiful.
All that is in the heavens and the earth magnifies Him;
He is the All-mighty, the All-wise.

– Qur'ān 59:22-24

Lā ilāha illā 'Llāh means there is no benefactor, no harmer, no exalter, no debaser, no giver, and no preventer except God.

– 'Abd Allāh Ibn 'Abbās [DAN/KS156]

I stand witness that there is no god but God, He is One and there is no partner with Him. He is the First, such that nothing was before Him. He is the Last, such that there is not limit for Him. Imagination cannot catch any of His qualities. Hearts cannot entertain belief about His nature. Analysis and division cannot be applied to Him. Eyes and hearts cannot compare Him.

– 'Alī ibn Abī Ṭālib [ALI/NB214]

Sufi Aphorisms

There is no He but Him, and no existent apart from Him.

– Afḍal ad-Dīn Kāshānī [KAZ/OL74]

The affirmation of Unity, in reality, is an attribute of the One whose Unity is affirmed, but in form it is an adornment of the affirmer.

– Abū Bakr ash-Shiblī [HAR/RS365]

Sufi Poetry

We imagined negation was affirmation,
our eye saw nonexistent things.
The eye that appeared in slumber—
how could it see other than fantasy and nonexistence?
– Jalāl ad-Dīn Rūmī [CHI/PL182]

As much as the banner of the world dances,
your eye sees a banner, but your spirit recognizes wind.
He who also knows the incapacity of wind
considers everything except the Presence of *but God* as *no god.*
– Jalāl ad-Dīn Rūmī [CHI/PL182]

Creation in unison screams,
"There is no one but the One."
The worldly clever is busy trying to
determine where he can cash in.
The ocean's bosom heaves in Love,
the floating twig takes the waves personally.
– Abū Sa'īd Ibn Abī'l-Khayr [ABR/NS71]

The joy and heartache of lovers is He,
the wages and salary for service is He.
If they were to gaze on other than the Beloved,
how could that be love? That would be idle fancy.
Love is that flame which, when it blazes up,
burns away all except the everlasting Beloved.
It slays "other than God" with the sword of *no god.*
Look carefully: After *no god* what remains?
There remains *but God*, the rest has gone.
Hail, O Love, great burner of all others!
It is He alone who is first and last,
all else grows up from the eye that sees double.
– Jalāl ad-Dīn Rūmī [CHI/SS69]

Sufi Instruction

To declare Divine Unity is to declare the uniqueness of the One Whose Unity is affirmed by attesting to His singularity in the perfection of His Oneness—that only He is the One that does not beget and is not begotten—and by denying all opposites, equals, and resemblances, without comparison, qualification, representation, or likening of Him to anything else. *Nothing is like unto Him, and He is the Hearing and Seeing* (42:11).

– Abū'l-Qāsim al-Junayd [HAR/RS364]

Reader, you may grasp His Oneness through your own oneness. Listen: you are one, and can come to know that One only through this one. Simple: One comes to know "Oneself." *You* and *it* are not involved in the slightest. The Profession of Unity [*lā ilāha illā 'Llāh*] is explained by this formula, though few indeed realize it: "Any individual number multiplied by oneness results in one individual number."

1x1 = 1

– Fakhr ad-Dīn 'Irāqī [CHI/DF99]

God is the witness who makes known that in His essence He is one, without partner, alone and without any like, enduring and without opposite, unique and without equal. He is one, pre-eternal with no first, from eternity without beginning, continuing in existence with no end, remaining to eternity without termination, stable and not cut short, lasting without being interrupted. He has not ceased, and will not cease, to be characterized by qualities of majesty. He is unaffected by passing away and separation through the interruption of enduring and the elapsing of appointed terms. Rather, He is the first and the last, the external and the internal, and He is knowing about everything.

– Abū Ḥāmid al-Ghazālī [WAT/IC73]

If you realize that "There is no god but God" surrounds all the meanings and that everything is enfolded in it, you must say that the reality of everything is "There is no god but God," or you would say—what someone said, "All the demands of the lovers exist in the essence of the Creator." Shaykh al-Harrāq said, "In Your Beauty are gathered all demands. We have no sight for other-than-You. Nothing I see is present when Your Face appears."

The gnostic is not a gnostic until he knows God in all aspects. The gnostic knows only one aspect which is the essence of the Real. *Wherever you turn, there is the Face of God* (2:115). Meaning that wherever you direct your senses in the sensory, wherever you turn your intellect in the intellectual field, or your illusion in the field of illusions, you will find the Face of God. In every place there is a source. And everything is "There is no god but God." This is why he says that it encompasses everything. Know that under "There is no god but God" is all existence in totality, all partial and all impermanent existence: or you can say, the existence of the Real and the existence of creation. The existence of creation comes under "There is no god," the meaning of which is that everything that is bereft of God is false and has no confirmation. The existence of the Real comes under "but God." All otherness comes under the first part and all praises come under the last part. And He is the First and the Last. If you understand this you will know the reality of beauty and majesty, and the gatherer of these two is the perfection that is nothing but the essence that requires Godhood. This means that existence is encompassed in the word of unity.

– Aḥmad al-'Alawī [MUN/KG50]

Know that there is no god other than Him. He is the Necessary Existent by His essence; the Unique, the One, the Able Sovereign, the Living and Sustaining, the Ancient without beginning, the Eternal without end. He has knowledge of all things, and power over all affairs. He does what He will; *nothing resembles Him, and He is the Hearer, the Seer* (42:11). Holy is He, and Exalted beyond being resembled or equaled, or having a partner or a minister. He is not subject to time, neither is He distracted by one affair away from another; He is neither subject to location nor affected by contingencies. He is absolutely Independent of all things, whatever their nature and however they are envisaged. All that is not Him needs Him in a way so total that it cannot even be conceived to diminish. He has created all creatures, as well as their actions, whether these be good or evil. *Blessed is God, the Best of Creators!* (23:14) *He guides whom He will, and leads whom He will astray* (35:8); *He gives to whom He will, and withholds from whom He will; He forgives whom He will and chastises whom He will* (2:284). *He is not questioned about what He does, rather, they are questioned* (21:23). He created and provided for them, sent down Books and Messengers to guide them, all out of grace and kindness. To confess His unity and obey Him is an obligation upon His servants, transmitted through His Messengers. He is obligated to none, for He is the Possessor and Master of all; none shares sovereignty with Him, and none has any right over Him. His promise to reward those who act well proceeds from His grace, and His warning that He will punish those who act with evil proceeds from His justice. Only the possessor of the abovementioned attributes is Divine; and, as these attributes undoubtedly belong to God, and not a single one, let alone them all, can possibly be attributed to any other, God alone is Divine, and no other divinity exists.

– 'Abdallah Ibn 'Alawī al-Ḥaddād [BAD/GS11-12]

The Contradiction of Affirmation

Sufi Aphorisms

Whosoever claims to affirm God's Oneness thereby sets up another beside Him.

– Ḥusayn Ibn Manṣūr al-Ḥallāj [LIN/SS128]

None truly affirms the Oneness of God, for whosoever affirms It thereby sets himself in contradiction with It. . . . He, He is the affirmation of His Oneness, and whosoever presumes to describe Him blasphemes [by creating a duality through the intrusion of his own person].

– 'Abd Allāh al-Harawī [LIN/SS128]

God Most High is the very one who Himself affirms His unity by the tongue of whatever of His creatures He wishes. If He Himself affirms His unity by my tongue, it is He and His affair. Otherwise, brother, I have nothing to do with affirming God's unity.

– Ḥusayn Ibn Manṣūr al-Ḥallāj [ERN/WE45]

The Contradiction of Denial

Sufi Instruction

One who affirms God's existence always manifests God, but one who denies God's existence is also a manifestor because affirmation is something that cannot be imagined without denial. It is flavorless and flat without it. For example, when a debater makes a proposition in a gathering, if there is no one to contest him, how can he prove it? What delight can his point have? Proof of affirmation is pleasant only in the face of denial. This world is a gathering for manifesting God: without both affirmer and denier the gathering would be dull, for both are manifestors of God.

– Jalāl ad-Dīn Rūmī [THA/SU184-185]

The *Shahādah* and Sincerity

Sufi Aphorisms

Lā ilāha illā 'Llāh is a remembrance, and the believer does not remember God except out of a sincere heart.

– Ibn 'Aṭā' Allāh al-Iskandarī [DAN/KS154]

No one says *no god but God* correctly unless he negates everything other than God from his soul and heart.

– Ibn 'Aṭā' Allāh al-Iskandarī [CHI/SS58]

There is no god is the path of "this affair" and *but God* is the final goal of "this affair." Until a person has been steadfast for years in *there is no god*, he will not reach *but God.*

– Abū Sa'īd Ibn Abī'l-Khayr [OKA/SG368]

Sufi Poetry

Before this there was one heart
But a thousand thoughts.
Now all is reduced to:
There is no god but God.

– Fakhr ad-Dīn 'Irāqī [CHI/DF180]

Love is the flame which, when it blazes,
consumes everything other than the Beloved.
The lover wields the sword of *No god*
in order to dispatch all but God.
Consider what remains after *No god*:
there remains *but God*, all the rest is gone.
Praise to you, O mighty Love,
destroyer of all other "gods."

– Jalāl ad-Dīn Rūmī [HEL/JR93]

Sufi Instruction

He to whom the mysteries of *lā ilāha illā 'Llāh* are revealed draws near to God, and his worship of God becomes sincere. He does not turn to anyone but to Him, nor does he have hope in or fear other than Him, nor does he see harm or benefit except as coming from Him. He abandons whosoever is not He and rids himself of inward and outward associationism (*shirk*).

– Ibn 'Aṭā' Allāh al-Iskandarī [DAN/KS140]

As God has said: *And He imposed on them the profession of true devotion* (48:26). That is the profession: "There is no god but God" [*lā ilāha illā 'Llāh*] with the stipulation that it must come from a heart that is truly devout, pure of everything apart from God, not like any statement heard from the mouths of the common folk. The wording may be the same in each case, but there is a difference in the meaning.

– 'Abd al-Qādir al-Jīlānī [JIL/BS31]

Every man has one heart and one heart cannot be occupied with two things at the same time. When it is occupied with one of two things, it is excluded from the other thing, and this to the extent of its preoccupation with the first. Thus, it behoves the one who says *lā ilāha illā 'Llāh* that he intend by *lā ilāha* the expulsion of what is other-than-God from his heart. When the heart is empty of what is other-than-God, and when the authority of God is present therein, its light shines with a complete radiance, and His possession of it is perfect.

– Ibn 'Aṭā' Allāh al-Iskandarī [DAN/KS137]

"*There is no God but God*" *is My fortress, and whoever enters My fortress becomes secure from My chastisement* (*ḥadīth qudsī*). Whoever comes into this fortress—He did not say "whoever mentions the name of this fortress." To say the name of the fortress is very easy. You say with the tongue, "I went into the fortress." Or you say, "I went to Damascus." If it's with the tongue, then in one blink you'll go to heaven and earth, you'll go to the Throne and the Footstool.

He [the Prophet] said, "Whoever says 'There is no god but God' purely and sincerely will enter the Garden." If you now sit and say it, your brain will dry out. He is one. Who are you? You're more than six thousand! Become one yourself—otherwise, what's His oneness to you? You are a hundred thousand dust motes, each dust mote taken by a caprice, each dust mote taken by an imagining.

"Purely" through his intention; "sincerely" through his activity. There's no need for the promise of entering the Garden. When he does that, he will be in the Garden itself.

– Shams-i-Tabrīzī [CHI/MR90-91]

The first covering is to say *lā ilāha illā 'Llāh* (There is no divinity but God) with your tongue. This is called "affirming the Oneness of God," because it is opposite to the doctrine of the Trinity which the Christians declare; but the affirmation might emanate from a hypocrite whose interior contradicts his exterior. The second covering is that one not have in one's heart any opposition to or rejection of the content of this formula. Rather, the literal meaning of the formula embraces both the adherence to it as a dogma and the belief in it. It is the profession of God's Oneness to which most people adhere. The theologians are the watchmen who protect this covering from the confusion of innovators. The third covering, which is the essence, is that one see all things from God Most High in a vision preventing one from giving undue consideration to intermediate causes; and to worship Him with a devotion that isolates Him from all else, so that one does not worship other-than-Him.

– Ibn 'Aṭā' Allāh al-Iskandarī [DAN/KS109-110]

O young man! You do not amount to anything. Islam [submission to the will of God] has not become a fact for you. Islam is the foundation upon which everything is built. The profession of faith [*Shahādah*] has not become completely real for you. You say: "There is no god but God" but you are lying. In your heart there is a whole collection of gods. Your fears of your ruler and of your local governor are gods. Your reliance on your earned income and your profit, on your power and your strength, on your hearing and your sight and your energy, all these are gods. Your ways of viewing creatures as the source of injury and benefit, of giving and withholding, are also gods. Many people talk about these things with their hearts, while making it appear that they are talking about the Lord of Truth. Their mentioning the Lord of Truth has become a habit for their tongues, not for their hearts.

When you say: "There is no god" (*lā ilāha*) it is an absolute negation (*nafy*), and "except God" (*illā 'Llāh*) is an absolute affirmation (*ithbāt*). You are asserting this as true of Him, not of any other than Him, so whenever your heart relies upon anything other than the Lord of Truth, you are making your affirmation falsely, for the thing you have relied upon has become your god (*ilāha*), regardless of outer appearances. It is the heart that is the believer, that is the monotheist, that is sincere, that is devout, that is pious, that is abstinent, that is convinced, that is experienced, that is effective, that is the leader while all the rest are its troops and its followers.

When you say: "There is no god but God," speak first with your heart and then with your tongue. Trust in Him and rely on Him, to the exclusion of any other than Him.

– 'Abd al-Qādir al-Jīlānī [JIL/SR113-114]

The *Shahādah* and Salvation

Foundational Sources

So whosoever disbelieves in false gods and believes in God, has laid hold of the most firm handle, unbreaking.

– Qur'ān 2:256

Lā ilāha illā 'Llāh is My fortress; whosoever enters My fortress is safe from My chastisement.

– *Ḥadīth Qudsī* [DAN/KS154]

If a person's last words are "There is no god but God," he will enter Paradise.

– *Ḥadīth* [FRI/SS58]

He who dies knowing that there is no god but God will enter the Garden.

– *Ḥadīth* [CHI/PK437]

The people most blest with my intercession shall be those who said *lā ilāha illā 'Llāh*, sincerely and without being prompted.

– *Ḥadīth* [BAD/LM65]

When a man says, "There is no god but God," the word comes on the leaf [of his book], and passes by [the records of his] sin, erasing them, until it finds a good deed similar to itself and then finally nestles down beside it.

– *Ḥadīth* [NAK/IS14]

The Messenger of God said, "Whosoever says *lā ilāha illā 'Llāh* sincerely, enters Paradise." He was asked, "O Messenger of God, how can one say the words sincerely?" He answered, "By keeping away from things forbidden." The Prophet said, "Be sincere! Even a little will suffice you!"

– *Ḥadīth* [DAN/KS150]

For the people of *lā ilāha illā 'Llāh*, there is neither loneliness at death nor at the Resurrection. It is as if I were looking at the people of *lā ilāha illā 'Llāh* at the moment of the Outcry, shaking off the dirt from their hair and saying, "Praise be to God who has put grief away from us."

– *Ḥadīth* [DAN/KS154]

The Prophet said to Abū Hurayrah, "O Abū Hurayrah, verily every good deed you perform shall be weighed on the Day of Resurrection except the testimony that 'There is no god but God,' as it cannot be weighed in the balance. For were it to be put on the balance of him who has confessed that formula sincerely, then even the seven heavens, the seven earths and what is on them could not counterbalance on the scales the weight of the formula 'There is no god but God.'"

– *Ḥadīth* [NAK/IS12]

If someone professes a hundred times every day, "There is no god but God, Who is alone; to Him belongs sovereignty and to Him belongs praise; He is powerful over everything," then he has as good as ransomed ten slaves, and a hundred good deeds are written down for him and a hundred evil deeds are erased from him, and this formula becomes a protection for him against Satan on that day, so that no one can bring a more meritorious deed than he did except by increasing the same act more than that.

– *Ḥadīth* [NAK/IS11]

Sufi Poetry

The *Shahādah* has saved millions from drowning
  and turned travelers into saints.
The *Shahādah* extinguishes hell,
  where an inescapable fire burns.
Through the *Shahādah*, the heavens are alive
  with blessings night and day.
There is no blessing like the *Shahādah*, Bāhū,
  in both resting places.

– Sulṭān Bāhū [ELI/DB125]

The Remembrance of the *Shahādah*

Foundational Sources

The most excellent recollection is saying "There is no god but God."

– *Ḥadīth* [REN/KG179]

The most meritorious thing that I and the previous prophets taught is the formula: "There is no god but God, Who alone is and has no associate."

– *Ḥadīth* [NAK/IS11]

The Prophet said, "Renew your faith." "How can we renew our faith?" they asked. The Prophet replied, "Say always, *lā ilāha illā 'Llāh.*"

– *Ḥadīth* [KAB/GB122]

He who remembers God much, God loves him. The night that I was enraptured to my Lord there passed by a man extinguished within the light of God's Throne. I asked, "Who is this, and is he an angel?" I was told "No," and I asked again, "Is it a Prophet?" I was told "No," and I said, "Who then?" It was said, "This is a man who, while he was in the world, his tongue was constantly moist with the mention of God, and his heart was attached to the mosques."

– *Ḥadīth* [KAB/GB142]

Sufi Stories

One day Shiblī was repeatedly uttering the word "God, God." An earnest young disciple addressed him, "Why do you not say 'There is no god but God'?" Shiblī sighed. "I am afraid," he explained, "that if I say 'no god' my breath may be stopped before I reach 'but God' and I shall be utterly desolated."

– Abū Bakr ash-Shiblī [ARB/MS282]

Sufi Poetry

There are no gates which open on your holy Essence:
    no one can know the depths of your perfection.
For travelers on the path to you there only remains
    to repeat and repeat *There is no god but God.*

– Awḥad ad-Dīn Kirmānī [WIL/HW123]

Sufi Instruction

With the *lā ilāha* (There is no god) I negate everything besides God, and with the *illā 'Llāh* (but God) I affirm the love of God in the heart.

– 'Alā' ad-Dawla as-Simnānī [ELI/TC24]

One of the sages said that it is not proper to invoke repetitively time after time except with a meaning which differs from the first one. He said, "The lowest level of the invocation is the one wherein every time one says, 'There is no divinity but God,' one expels from the heart whatever is other-than-God. But if one pays attention to it, then one has as much as ascribed to it the position of deity."

– Ibn 'Aṭā' Allāh al-Iskandarī [DAN/KS70]

As for the second invocation, it is *lā ilāha illā 'Llāh* (There is no divinity but God), and its textual proof is in the words of God: *Know that there is no divinity but God. . .* (47:19); and in the words of the

Prophet, "The best thing that I and the Prophets before me have said is 'There is no divinity but God.'"

In this Testimony there is the negation (*nafy*) of any divinity apart from God and the affirmation (*ithbāt*) of the divinity of God Most High. No worship exists without there being implicit in it the meaning of "There is no divinity but God." Thus, ritual purity implies the negation of uncleanness and the affirmation of ritual purity. In almsgiving, there is negation of the love of money and affirmation of the love of God; there is the manifestation of being in no need of the world, of being in need of God Most High, and of being satisfied with Him.

Also, for the heart filled with that which is other-than-God, there must be a formula of negation to negate the alterities [othernesses]. When the heart becomes empty, the *minbar* [pulpit] of the Divine Oneness is placed therein and the sultan of gnosis sits upon it. In general, only the best of things, the most universally beneficial, and the most significant are placed therein, because they are the prototypes against which the heart measures their opposites. Enough power must exist in that locus of the heart to permit it to confront every opposite. For that reason the Prophet said, "The best thing that I and the Prophets before me have said is 'There is no divinity but God.'"

– Ibn 'Aṭā' Allāh al-Iskandarī [DAN/KS89-90]

The *Shahādah* and *Fanā'-Baqā'*

Sufi Aphorisms

The sign of the reality of one's profession of Unity is to forget professing the Unity. That is, he who performs a real declaration of oneness becomes one.

– Ibn 'Aṭā' Allāh al-Iskandarī [HAR/RS368]

The affirmation of unity is a spiritual condition in which all forms vanish and into which all knowledges are incorporated, and God Most High becomes what He always was.

– Abū'l-Qāsim al-Junayd [HAR/RS365]

Sufi Poetry

He said *No god*, then He said *but God*:
No became *but God* and Oneness blossomed forth.

– Jalāl ad-Dīn Rūmī [CHI/PL182]

This world is negation, so seek in affirmation:
Your form is nothing, so seek in your meaning!
– Jalāl ad-Dīn Rūmī [CHI/PL182]

Oh spirit, come and acknowledge! Oh body, go and deny!
Oh *no god*, take me to the gallows, for you drag to *but God*!
– Jalāl ad-Dīn Rūmī [CHI/PL182]

Beyond denial and affirmation lies a desert;
It is a place of profit for members of this group.
When the lover arrives here, he turns to nothing:
Not denial, not affirmation, not even "you" exist there!
– Sharaf ad-Dīn Manīrī [JAC/HL152]

The one who knows the secret
is freed from his self
and lives in the company of the Beloved.
Negate your own existence,
negate the self
and declare the Being of the Beloved.
This is what *lā ilāha illā 'Llāh* means.
– Abū Sa'īd Ibn Abī'l-Khayr [ABR/NS13]

"There is no god but God"—
the NO is affirmation
because of the BUT.
What is united with us
will never
be cut off:
Where did the atom "go"
when it reached
the sun?
What became of the drop
when it fell
in the sea?
– Awḥad ad-Dīn Kirmānī [WIL/HW133]

Sufi Instruction

With *no god* the practitioner negates other than the Real, and with *but God* he affirms the Presence of Exaltation. When he does this constantly and clings to it, the spirit's attachment to other than God is gradually cut with the scissors of *no god*. The beauty of *but God*'s authority discloses itself from behind the Pavilion of Exaltation. In keeping with the promise, *Remember Me, and I will remember you* (2:152), the remembrance is disengaged from the clothing of letters and sound. The specific characteristics of *Everything is perishing but His Face* (28:88) become evident in the disclosure of the light of Divinity's magnificence.

– Najm ad-Dīn Rāzī [CHI/SS58]

Junayd was asked about the profession of Unity of the spiritual elite. He said, "It means that the servant is but a phantom shape before God, glory to Him. Over him flow the currents of God's direction of the changing play of His power. Through passing away from himself, the call of the world to him, and his response with his own being and individuality, he comes to reside in the depths of the seas of God's Unity. Through leaving his own sensation and action in order to be maintained by the Truth according to His wish, he comes to reside in real closeness to Him. The end of the servant returns to his beginning, so that he becomes as he was before he was."

– Abū'l-Qāsim al-Junayd [HAR/RS365]

For legal scholars, denial (*nafy*) comes after affirmation (*ithbāt*), whereas lexicographers state that affirmation comes after negation. For a Sufi, both denial and affirmation are idolatry. The reason is that affirmation requires "three" if it is to be a complete affirmation: the thing affirmed, the affirmer, and the act of affirmation. Denial also needs three things for its completion: the act of denial, the one denying, and the thing denied—yet anyone who talks even of two is a polytheist and unbeliever, so how could anyone who sees six be a sincere and orthodox believer? Why are you astonished? Any "other" simply does not exist! Who, then, denies? And since you yourself do not exist, how can you affirm anything?

– Sharaf ad-Dīn Manīrī [JAC/HL153]

When you say "there is no god but God," it is necessary that you be totally aware and convinced that you, your mother, your father, all of humanity, all the universe and what it contains, from the smallest atom and living creature to the furthest of stars—all are created by Him. He is the owner of your body and mind, the air you breathe, the food you consume, and everything you own. . . . Each human being and every living thing is dependent upon and in need of another, and that other is dependent upon a third. This chain of dependence goes on and on until it reaches the One God upon whom all depend. That is another fact we must realize in our faith in One God: no part of our existence, or the existence of all and everything, is independent of Him. To say *lā ilāha illā 'Llāh* with this kind of conviction is to declare the unity of all and everything with its Creator, as God has ordained. Although the Creator bears no resemblance to His creation, yet His creation cannot be conceived of as separate from Him.

– Mehmet Efendi Birgīvi [BAY/PM35-36]

Other lights are lights derived from the light that is adjacent to Him, not from His own Essence. Thus, the face of every possessor of a face is toward Him and turned in His direction. *Whithersoever you turn, there is the face of God* (2:115). Hence, there is no god but He. For "god" is an expression for that toward which a face turns through worship and becoming godlike. Here I mean the faces of the hearts, since they are lights. Indeed, just as there is no god but He, so also there is no he but He, because "he" is an expression for whatever may be pointed to, and there is no pointing to anything but Him. Or, rather, whenever you point to something, in reality you are pointing to Him. If you do not know this, that is because you are heedless of "the Reality of realities" that we mentioned.

One does not point to the light of the sun but, rather, to the sun. In the obvious sense of this example, everything in existence is related to God just as light is related to the sun. Therefore, "There is no god but God" is the declaration of God's unity of the common people, while "There is no he but He" is the declaration of God's unity of the elect, since this declaration of God's unity is more complete, more specific, more comprehensive, more worthy, and more precise. It is more able to make its possessor enter into sheer singularity and utter oneness.

– Abū Ḥāmid al-Ghazālī [BUC/NL20]

It should be known, at the very beginning, that belief in the unity of God can be divided into four stages. In the first of these a person proclaims *There is no god but God!* (47:19) but his heart is devoid of faith. Such belief is hypocrisy and will prove profitless in the next life. In the second stage a person both proclaims "There is no god but God!" and believes in his heart that this is so. This type of belief can be either conventional—as is true for ordinary people—or supported by rational proofs—as is the case of the learned. This is the way belief normally manifests itself. In truth it can be said: Come, open your eyes and see that each particle of dust, if you look carefully, contains a world-revealing cup. Sufis say that such faith prevents people from falling into crass polytheism and saves them from languishing eternally in hell. It also ensures entrance into paradise. Although this type of belief is more beneficial and enduring than the first, there is still an element of instability about it. The highest form of belief is for you, my friend, not this, which is fit for old women!

The third stage is said to be reached when a person's soul is illuminated in such a way that he is able to perceive every action flowing from a single source and deriving from a single agent. This firm belief is different from the faith of common people and the faith of the learned, both of which are constricted. This elevates the heart. It is the contemplation of a light that effaces creatures! . . . He is a Sufi who, in this stage, sees creatures and experiences the Creator, in the sense that he perceives that they all come from Him. This very discrimination, however, indicates that the state of complete unification has not yet been attained.

Sufi masters are of the opinion that, in the fourth stage, such a surfeit of the dazzling divine light becomes manifest to the pilgrim that every single existing particle that lies within his vision becomes concealed in the very luster of that light just as particles in the air are lost to sight on account of the brightness of the light emanating from the sun. This occurs not because the particles have ceased to exist but rather because the intensity of the sunlight makes it impossible that anything other than this concealment should result. In the same way, it is not true that a person becomes God—for God is infinitely greater than any man—nor has the person really ceased to exist, for ceasing to exist is one thing, and becoming lost to view quite another!

> Before your Unique Being, there is neither old nor new:
> Everything is nothing, nothing at all! Yet He is what He is.
> How then can we remain separate from You?
> When "I" and "You" have passed away,
> God alone will remain!

– Sharaf ad-Dīn Manīrī [JAC/HL12-13]

III. Discernment of Unity: The Manifold Aspects of *Tawḥīd*

Unity / Uniqueness
Metaphysics: No existence but God

	Transcendent Pole			
Microcosmic Pole	The Only Worshipped *subjective Totality* (*entry to self-perishing*)	Independent *causally Independent* ↴ The Source of All ↴ ↳ The End of All ↵ *causally Encompassing*	Beyond Comprehension *objective Nonmanifest*	*Macrocosmic Pole*
	In Relation to the Self *subjective Disclosure* Intimately Present *objective Subject* Only Witness / Actor *subjective Subject*	→ "... *upon the horizons and in themselves* ..." ← → ← ↔ All-Witnessing *Subject of Object* ↔	In Relation to Creation *objective Disclosure* All-Encompassing *objective Object* Only Witnessed *subjective Object*	
	Immanent Pole			

The Perishing of All Otherness
Realization: No self but God

III. Discernment of Unity: The Metaphysics of *Tawḥīd*

Overview: *Tawḥīd*

The doctrinal content of the *Shahādah* is, as we have noted in the introduction, signified by the Arabic term *tawḥīd* (unity), a word that literally means "to make one" or "to acknowledge oneness." This definition points to a telling ambiguity at the heart of the very doctrine of unity. God is One, reality is one, yet the world is—to all immediate and apparent evidence—many. How can God be One and yet the world be many? For God is the Real and existence is, necessarily, an expression and aspect of that reality. Unity *is*, and yet that unity must be discerned, acknowledged, asserted. This is the task of the metaphysical elucidation of *tawḥīd.*

The Sufi tradition, in elucidating the nature of unity in apparent multiplicity, speaks of two distinct ontological pairs: the first, that of transcendence and immanence, describes God in relation to the world, at once utterly apart from it and fully bound up with it; the second, that of the microcosm and the macrocosm, describes the fundamental division of the world itself into human subjectivity on the one hand and the objective cosmos on the other. With respect to the Divine immanence in the macrocosm, God stands as objectively disclosed in relation to the whole of creation. With respect to that same immanence in the microcosm, God stands as subjectively disclosed in relation to the human self. Both of these disclosures are jointly indicated in the important Qur'ānic verse, "We shall show them Our signs upon the horizons and in themselves until it is clear to them that He is the Real" (41:53), pointing to the Divine disclosure (*tajallī*) to both the cosmic macrocosm and human microcosm.

The objective disclosure of God in the macrocosm may be understood in two further, subjacent modes: objectively, God is all-encompassing, as there is no place in creation where God is not found; subjectively, God is the only witnessed in which everything in creation is revealed as the Face of God. Similarly, the subjective disclosure of God in the microcosm may be understood in two further, subjacent modes: objectively, God is intimately present, as He is closer to the human self than his jugular vein;[1] subjectively, God is the only witness and actor in which even the self's witnessing consciousness and volition is not other than God's. Further, God as all-witnessing is at once both unique Subject and only Object, for He is the only knower and only known.

Turning from the Divine immanence to the Divine transcendence, we may again consider this in relation to both microcosm and macrocosm. Objectively, in relation to the creation, God is beyond comprehension and apart from manifestation. Subjectively, in relation to the human self, God's transcendence entails that He is properly the only to be worshipped, a principle extended by the Sufi tradition such that one's heart and attention should be wholly given to God, in turn serving as an opening to the experience of the passing away of the self (*fanā'*) and the subsistence of God (*baqā'*). The means by which God may be the only worshipped is precisely the discipline of invocation (*dhikr*). The Divine transcendence, in relation to both microcosm and macrocosm, is at once independent of all things as well as both the source from which they have originated and the end to which they must return.

Ultimately, all of these aspects of unity in apparent multiplicity are necessarily subsumed in the sole reality of God, for just as, in the metaphysical insight into the nature of creation there is no existence but God, so also, in the interior realization of the human soul, there is no self but God.

Unity and Uniqueness

Foundational Sources

God the One, the Omnipotent.

– Qur'ān 12:39

Do not dispute with the People of the Book[2] save in the fairer manner,

[1] This is an allusion to the Qur'ānic passage, "We indeed created man; and We know what his soul whispers within him, and We are nearer to him than his jugular vein" (50:16).

[2] *Ahl al-kitāb*, literally "people of the book," the Qur'ānic expression used to describe people to whom a holy book has been revealed. At the beginning of Islamic history the term was used in reference to the Christians, Jews, and the Sabeans and later, with the conquest of Persia, to Zoroastrians. But the principle was applied afresh whenever Muslims encountered a genuine living tradition so that later Hindus and Buddhists

except for those of them that do wrong; and say, "We believe in what has been sent down to us, and what has been sent down to you; our God and your God is One, and to Him we have surrendered."

– Qur'ān 29:46

Say [O Muḥammad]: "I am only a warner. There is not any god but God, the One, the Omnipotent, Lord of the heavens and earth, and of what is between them, the All-mighty, the All-forgiving."

– Qur'ān 38:65

Say [O Muḥammad]: "I am only a mortal, like you are. To me it has been revealed that your God is One God; so go straight with Him, and ask for His forgiveness."

– Qur'ān 41:6

Say: "He, God, is One;
God—the Eternally Sufficient and Infinite Plenitude.
He has neither begotten nor was begotten,
and comparable to Him there is none."

– Qur'ān 112:1-4

Whoever says: "There is no god but God" and "God is greater," his Lord confirms his truthfulness and says: "There is no god but Me" and "I am the Great." And if he says: "There is no god but God alone," God says: "There is no god but Me alone." And if he says: "There is no god but God alone; He has no partner," God says: "There is no god but Me alone, and I have no partner." And if he says: "There is no god except God; His is the Kingdom and His the Praise," God says: "There is no god but Me; Mine is the Kingdom, and Mine the praise." And if he says: "There is no god but God, and there is no power nor strength save through God," God says: "There is no god but Me, and there is no power nor strength save through Me."

– *Ḥadīth Qudsī* [HIR/DS54]

God was, and there was nothing other than He, and He is now, and there is nothing.

– *Ḥadīth* [CHI/SD435]

were also described by certain Islamic spiritual authorities as "people of the book." See Seyyed Hossein Nasr, *Ideals and Realities of Islam* (San Francisco, CA: Aquarian Press, 1994), p.189.

He is One but not by the first in counting; is Creator but not through activity or labor; is Hearer but not by means of any physical organ; is Looker but not by a stretching of eyelids; is Witness but not by nearness; is Distinct but not by measurement of distance; is Manifest but not by seeing; is Hidden but not by subtlety of form. He is Distinct from things because He overpowers them and exercises might over them, while things are distinct from Him because of their subjugation to Him and their turning towards Him.

He who describes Him limits Him. He who limits Him numbers Him. He who numbers Him rejects His eternity. He who said "how" sought a description for Him. He who said "where" bounded Him. He is the Knower even though there be nothing to be known. He is the Sustainer even though there be nothing to be sustained. He is the Powerful even though there be nothing to be overpowered.

– 'Alī ibn Abī Ṭālib [ALI/NB310]

Sufi Aphorisms

Tawḥīd is a reality in which the traces disappear and the signs fade away, and God is as He always was.

– Abū'l-Qāsim al-Junayd [KAD/AJ68-69]

He alone is the Observer, He alone is the Observed!
There is none but He in the world of existence.

– Muḥyī ad-Dīn Ibn al-'Arabī [VAL/QS149]

What is there in the two worlds except the Single Essence?
Nothing exists in the entire universe except He!

– 'Abd ar-Raḥmān Jāmī [VAL/CD160]

God is not veiled from you by some reality existing apart from Him, since there is no reality outside of Him; what veils Him from you is but the illusion that there can be a reality apart from Him.

– Ibn 'Aṭā' Allāh al-Iskandarī [BUR/LS7]

Whether one is inclined to evil or good, whether one is an inmate of a cloister or a monk in a monastery, from the point of view of "form," everyone is other than He. But from the point of view of reality everything is He and none other than He!

– 'Abd ar-Raḥmān Jāmī [VAL/QS110]

Sufi Poetry

All thou beholdest is the act of one
    In solitude, but closely veiled is He.
Let Him but lift the screen, no doubt remains:
    The forms are vanished, He alone is all.

– Ibn al-Fāriḍ [STE/SW13]

Sufi Instruction

Oh God, verily we affirm Your oneness but do not limit You, we believe in You but do not conceive of You in a specific form, we worship You but do not conceive of You as resembling anything. Furthermore, we believe that one who conceives of You as resembling what You have created will never know the difference between the Creator and creation. *Say:* "*He is God the One; God the Incomparable; He begets not, nor is He begotten, and there is none like unto Him*" (112:1-4).

– Abū Madyan [COR/AM50]

In Relation to Creation

Foundational Sources

God is the Light of the heavens and the earth.

– Qur'ān 24:35

We are through Him and for Him.

– *Ḥadīth* [CHI/SD441]

Praise be to God Who lies inside all hidden things, and towards Whom all open things guide. He cannot be seen by the eye of an onlooker, but the eye which does not see Him cannot deny Him while the mind that proves His existence cannot perceive Him. He is so high in sublimity that nothing can be more sublime than He, while in nearness, He is so near that no one can be nearer than He. But His sublimity does not put Him at a distance from anything of His creation, nor does His nearness bring them on equal level to Him. He has not informed human wit about the limits of His qualities. Nevertheless, He has not prevented it from securing essential knowledge of Him. So He is such that all signs of existence stand witness for Him till the denying mind also believes in Him. He is sublime beyond what is described by those who liken

Him to things or those who deny Him.

–'Alī ibn Abī Ṭālib [ALI/NB181]

Sufi Aphorisms

The water takes on the color of the cup.

– Abū'l-Qāsim al-Junayd [CHI/SD441]

They are neither He nor other than He.

– "Kullabite" formula of the Ash'arite theologians [CHI/SD440]

There is nothing in *wujūd* [existence, being] but God.

– Abū Ḥāmid al-Ghazālī [CHI/SD440]

The Real becomes clear when the designation dissolves.

– Ibn al-'Arīf [CHI/SD439]

There is nothing in possibility more wondrous than what is.

– Abū Ḥāmid al-Ghazālī [CHI/PK439]

Sufi Instruction

The created cosmos is all darkness. It is illumined only by the manifestation of God in it. He who sees the world and does not contemplate Him in it or by it or before it or after it, is in need of illumination and is veiled from the suns of gnosis beneath the clouds of created things.

– Ibn 'Aṭā' Allāh al-Iskandarī [LEW/WS196]

Sufi Poetry

And in everything there is a witness for Him
Which points to the fact that He is One.

– Abū'l-Atāhiya [SCH/MD146]

Know that the world of created things
Is like pure and limpid water
In which shine the attributes
Of the Omnipotent One.

– Jalāl ad-Dīn Rūmī [HAR/TR11-12]

The world is no more than a manifestation
of the uniqueness of the Beloved;
But for the Beauty that seems its own awareness,

we ourselves would not exist.
Each place and instance sings, in varying measure,
a song of being and nonbeing; it is fruitless.
Wherever His footprint reveals itself,
that handful of dust is the treaty
for the integrity of the two worlds.
– Mīrzā Ghālib [STE/SW17]

If You are Everything
then who are all these people?
And if I am nothing
what's all this noise about?
You are Totality,
everything is You. Agreed.
Then that which is "other-than-You"—
what is it?
Oh, indeed I know:
Nothing exists but You;
but tell me:
Whence this confusion?
– Fakhr ad-Dīn 'Irāqī [CHI/DF99]

In Relation to the Self

Foundational Sources

We shall show them Our signs upon the horizons and in themselves, until it is clear to them that He is the Real.
– Qur'ān 41:53

My heavens and My earth embrace Me not, but the heart of My believing servant does embrace Me.
– *Ḥadīth Qudsī* [CHI/PK438]

He who knows himself knows his Lord.
[alternatively: He who recognizes himself recognizes his Lord]
– *Ḥadīth* [CHI/SD436]

Sufi Aphorisms

The soul is an ocean without shore.
– Muḥyī ad-Dīn Ibn al-'Arabī [CHI/PK439]

Sufi Poetry

If you say, "We are one,"
you have spoken the truth,
and if you say, "Not one are we,"
that is no lie.

– Muḥyī ad-Dīn Ibn al-'Arabī [CHI/SD236]

Hold to the reins of Love and don't be afraid.
Hold to the real behind the false and don't be afraid.
You must know that the Beloved you seek is none other than you.
Hold to this truth and don't be afraid.

– Jalāl ad-Dīn Rūmī [STA/RA157]

You are my face: no wonder I don't see You:
such closeness is a mystifying veil.
You are my reason: it's no wonder I don't see You,
because of all this perplexity of thought.
You are nearer to me than my jugular vein.[3]

– Jalāl ad-Dīn Rūmī [HEL/JR140]

If you keep seeking the jewel of understanding,
then you are a mine of understanding in the making.
If you live to reach the Essence one day,
then your life itself is an expression of the Essence.
Know that in the final analysis you are that
which you search for.

– Abū Sa'īd Ibn Abī'l-Khayr [ABR/NS64]

All-Encompassing

Foundational Sources

To God belong the East and the West; whithersoever you turn, there is the Face of God; God is All-embracing, All-knowing.

– Qur'ān 2:115

To God belongs all that is in the heavens and in the earth, and God encompasses everything.

– Qur'ān 4:126

[3] Alluding to the Qur'ān 50:16 (see footnote 1 of this chapter).

Are they not in doubt touching the encounter with their Lord? Does He not encompass everything?

– Qur'ān 41:54

He is the First and the Last, the Manifest and the Nonmanifest; He is Knower of all things.

– Qur'ān 57:3

If you let down a man with a rope to the lowest earth, he will fall upon God.

– *Ḥadīth* [CHI/SD438]

Sufi Aphorisms

A disciple asked Abū-Sa'īd, "Where shall we seek Him?" Abū Sa'īd replied, "Where did you look that you did not find Him?"

– Abū Sa'īd Ibn Abī'l-Khayr [JAM/UC16]

Sufi Poetry

The peerless God has made all the six directions a theater
for the display of His signs to the clear-seeing,
so that, whatever animal or plant they look upon,
they may feed on the meadows of divine Beauty.
And so He said to the mystic companions,
Wherever you turn, there is the Face of God (2:115).
If in thirst you drink some water from a cup,
you are beholding God in the water.
The one who is not a lover of God
sees his own image in the water, O you of insight;
but since the lover's image has disappeared in the Beloved,
whom now should he behold in the water? Tell me that!

– Jalāl ad-Dīn Rūmī [HEL/JR179]

Say: "Allāh!" and let go of existence with all it contains,
if you desire the attainment of perfection.
For everything other than God, were you to realize it,
is nothing, whether in part or as a whole.
And know that you and all the worlds,
were it not for Him, would be obliterated and destroyed.
As for the one who has no existence in and of himself,
were it not for God, "his" existence would be utterly impossible.
The gnostics have been annihilated—they perceive

nothing but the Imperious, the Most Exalted.
They see what is other than Him destroyed in actuality,
in the present, in the past, and in the future.
So look, either with your intellect or with your eye,
do you see anything but an action among acts?
Examine the highest and lowest levels of existence
with a view that is supported by demonstrable proof,
And you will find that all which exists alludes to His Majesty
with the language of experience or the language of speech.
He is the Encompasser of all things, from the highest to
the lowest, and their Originator, beyond compare.

– Abū Madyan [COR/AM168]

Sufi Instruction

Nothing is before God and nothing is after Him; nothing other than He Himself is above Him or below Him. All that which is before or after Him, whether hidden or apparent, is One—His right and left, up and down, near and far, are all One. It is for this reason that He cannot be said to have any place or direction.

– Shāh Dā'ī Shīrāzī [POU/KL72]

Intimately Present

Foundational Sources

When My servants question you concerning Me—surely I am near.

– Qur'ān 2:186

We are nearer to him than the jugular vein.

– Qur'ān 50:16

And We are nearer to him than you are, but you do not see.

– Qur'ān 56:85

He is with you wherever you are; and God sees the things you do.

– Qur'ān 57:4

Sufi Aphorisms

We drown in an endless ocean, yet our lips are parched with thirst.

– Aḥmad al-Ghazālī [WIL/DU104-106]

Sufi Poetry

And He is with you (57:4) means He is searching with you.
He is nearer to you than yourself. Why look outside?
Become like melting snow; wash yourself of yourself.
With love your inner voice will find a tongue
growing like a silent white lily in the heart.
– Jalāl ad-Dīn Rūmī [HEL/LS35]

Do not look for God,
Look for the one
looking for God.
But why look at all?—
He is not lost,
He is right here,
Closer than your own breath.
– Jalāl ad-Dīn Rūmī [STA/GB85]

The Beloved was face to face,
and I knew it not.
He was intimately close to me,
and I knew it not.
I said: "Seek"—
but I had already arrived!
I myself was scattering,
and I knew it not.
– Sharaf ad-Dīn Manīrī [JAC/QG232]

The way of union
is not what we thought.
The world of soul
is not what we imagined.
The Fountain of Eternal Life
is closer than you think.
The Water of Life
is in this very house—
but still, we need to drink it.
– Ṣadr ad-Dīn Qūnawī [FID/LA34]

Pilgrims on the way! Where are you?
Here is the beloved, here!
Your beloved lives next door

wall to wall.
Why do you wander
round and round the desert?
If you look into the face of Love
    and not just at its superficial form
you yourselves become the house of God
    and are its lords.
Ten times
you trod the trek unto that house [the Ka'ba].
    For once
    come into this house
    climb onto this roof.
That sweet house of sanctity—
you have described its features in detail
    but now give me some indication
    of the features of its Lord.
If you have seen that garden,
where is your bouquet of souvenirs?
If you are from God's sea,
where is your mother pearl of soul?
And yet, may all your troubles
    bring you treasure!
Too bad that you yourselves are veiling
    the treasures hid within.

– Jalāl ad-Dīn Rūmī [LEW/SS26]

Only Witnessed

Foundational Sources

And they shall know that God is the Evident Real.

– Qur'ān 24:25

Worship God as if you see Him, for if you do not see Him, He sees you.[4]

– *Ḥadīth* [CHI/SD434]

I have never seen anything without seeing God before it.

– Abū Bakr aṣ-Ṣiddīq [CHI/SD437]

[4] In both respects, this is the actual state of affairs.

I have never seen anything without seeing God with it.
– 'Umar ibn al-Khattāb [CHI/SD437]

I have never looked at a single thing without God being nearer to me than it.
– Abū 'Ubaidah [LIN/SS128]

Sufi Aphorisms

I never saw anything except God.
– Abū Bakr ash-Shiblī [SCH/MD147]

I never saw anything without seeing God therein.
– Muḥammad ibn Wasi' [SCH/MD147]

Had I been obliged to see other-than-Him, I would not have been able to do it since there is nothing else with Him, so how can I see it with Him?
– Mulay al-'Arabī ad-Darqāwī [ABD/DW155]

Whithersoever ye turn, there is the Face of God (2:109). That Face is ever current, uninterrupted, and abiding, never ceasing. True lovers sacrifice themselves to this Face and seek nothing in return.
– Jalāl ad-Dīn Rūmī [THA/SU21]

When you look with the eye of your intellect, you will not find anything but Him pictured in bodily forms. Yet when you seek Reality from other than Him, the transformation of your ignorance remains incomplete.
– Abū Madyan [COR/AM174]

Sufi Poetry

Rose and mirror and sun and moon—where are they?
Wherever we looked, there was always Thy face.
– Mīr Taqī Mīr [SCH/MD289]

Each soul is created to serve as your mirror.
All things in the two worlds are only your mirrors.
The heart is the mirror of your most royal beauty—
and both of these worlds are the case of that mirror.
– Najm ad-Dīn Rāzī [FID/LA72]

How can it be conceived that something veils Him,
since He is the one who manifests everything?
How can it be conceived that something veils Him,
since He is the one who is manifest through everything?
How can it be conceived that something veils Him,
since He is the one who is manifest in everything?
How can it be conceived that something veils Him,
since He is the Manifest to everything?
How can it be conceived that something veils Him,
since He was the Manifest before the existence of everything?
How can it be conceived that something veils Him,
since He is more manifest than anything?
How can it be conceived that something veils Him,
since He is the One alongside of whom there is nothing?
How can it be conceived that something veils Him,
since He is nearer to you than anything else?
How can it be conceived that something veils Him,
since were it not for Him the existence of everything would not be manifest?
It is a marvel how Being has been manifested in non-being,
and how the contingent has been established alongside of Him who possesses the attribute of Eternity!

– Ibn 'Aṭā' Allāh al-Iskandarī [KAZ/JR152-153]

Sufi Instruction

I was in a state of remembrance and my eyes were lowered and I heard a voice say: *He is the First and the Last and the Outwardly Manifest and the Inwardly Hidden* (57:3). I remained silent, and the voice repeated it a second time, and then a third, whereupon I said: "As to *the First*, I understand, and as to *the Last*, I understand, and as to *the Inwardly Hidden*, I understand, but as to *the Outwardly Manifest*, I see nothing but created things." Then the voice said: "If there were any outwardly manifest other than Himself I should have told thee." In that moment I realized the whole hierarchy of Absolute Being.

– Mulay al-'Arabī ad-Darqāwī [LIN/SS131]

Only Witness

Sufi Aphorisms

None knows God but God.

– Abū Sa'īd al-Kharrāz, et al. [CHI/PK438]

Sufi Poetry

None has affirmed the Unity of the One,
since all who affirm it deny it.
The *tawḥīd* of him who speaks of His description
is a loan, made null by the One.
His *tawḥīd* of Himself is His *tawḥīd*—
he who describes it has gone astray.

– Khwāja ʿAbd Allāh Anṣārī [MUR/TI49]

None recognizes God but God. None says God but God. He who supposes that he has expressed *tawḥīd* has associated others with God.

Does anyone exist to whom reason may say "O He"
other than Thou?
Does any have grandeur and power
other than Thou?
What should I say about Thee?
What can I say?
Thou speakest, Thou hearest—where is a thou-ness
other than Thou?

Glory be to Him who expresses His own *tawḥīd* with the tongue of His servant!

– Naṣīr ad-Dīn Qūnawī [CHI/FP70]

Only Actor

Foundational Sources

[O Muḥammad] you did not throw when you threw, but God threw.
– Qur'ān 8:17

God says on the tongue of His servant, "God hears him who praises Him."

– *Ḥadīth Qudsī* [CHI/SD435]

There is no power and no strength save in God, the All-high, the Tremendous.

– *Ḥadīth* [CHI/PK439]

Sufi Aphorisms

There is no actor save God.

– Abū Ḥāmid al-Ghazālī [CHI/SD440]

Lovers themselves do not seek—
in the whole world, there is no seeker but He.

– Jalāl ad-Dīn Rūmī [CHI/PL210]

Those who regard things as determined by God turn to God in everything.

– Abū'l-Ḥusayn an-Nūrī [NIC/RM132]

Sufi Poetry

See how the hand is invisible while the pen is writing;
the horse careening, yet the rider unseen;
the arrow flying, but the bow out of sight;
individual souls existing,
while the Soul of souls is hidden.

– Jalāl ad-Dīn Rūmī [HEL/RD134]

You are the instrument of an act,
nothing else.
Of the act's Agent,
you are nothing but a sign.
You are a world,
and the goal of the world is you.
But look carefully—
in the midst of all this you are nothing.

– Naṣīr ad-Dīn Qūnawī [CHI/FP79]

None lives but his life is from Mine,
and every willing soul is obedient to My will;
And there is no speaker but tells his tale with My words,
nor any seer but sees with the sight of Mine eye;
And no silent listener but hears with My hearing,
nor any one that grasps but with My strength and might;
And in the whole creation
there is none save Me that speaks or sees or hears.

– Ibn al-Fāriḍ [NIC/IP28]

All-Witnessing

Foundational Sources

And He has knowledge of everything.
– Qur'ān 2:29

And fear God, and know that God has knowledge of everything.
– Qur'ān 2:231

From God nothing whatever is hidden in heaven and earth.
– Qur'ān 3:5

You [God] are the Knower of the things unseen.
– Qur'ān 5:109

He is the Knower of the Unseen and the visible; He is the All-wise, the All-aware.
– Qur'ān 6:74

God is All-hearing, All-seeing.
– Qur'ān 22:61; 40:20

Our Lord, You embrace every thing in mercy and knowledge.
– Qur'ān 40:7

Suffices it not as to your Lord, that He is witness over everything?
– Qur'ān 41:53

God encompasses everything in knowledge.
– Qur'ān 65:12

Shall He not know, He who created? And He is the All-subtle, the All-aware.
– Qur'ān 67:14

My knowledge and your knowledge fall short of God's knowledge.
– *Ḥadīth* [CHI/SD439]

Sufi Aphorisms

There is no existence other than God, and the knowledge of Him and the knower of Him are not other than He.
– Badr ad-Dīn as-Simawnī [BAY/PB13]

Sufi Poetry

How can I not know You when You are the Outwardly Manifest, making Yourself known to me in every thing?

How can I realize Your Unity
when in Uniqueness I have no existence?

How can I not realize Your Unity
when Union is the very secret of servanthood?

Glory be to You! There is no god but You! No one but You can realize Your Unity, for You are as You are in pre-eternity without beginning and post-eternity without end. In reality, no other than You can realize Your Unity, and in sum, none knows You except You. You hide and You manifest—yet You do not hide from Yourself nor do You manifest to other than Yourself, for You are You. There is no god but You.
– Muḥyī ad-Dīn Ibn al-'Arabī [BEN/SD44]

Beyond Comprehension

Foundational Sources

He knows what lies before them and what is after them, and they comprehend not anything of His knowledge save such as He wills.
– Qur'ān 2:255

Vision attains Him not, but He attains all vision; He is the All-subtle, the All-aware.
– Qur'ān 6:103

Nothing is like Him, and He is the All-hearing, the All-seeing.
– Qur'ān 42:11

O God, increase my bewilderment in Thee!
– *Ḥadīth* [CHI/PK439]

Reflect upon all things, but reflect not upon God's Essence.
– *Ḥadīth* [CHI/PK439]

The incapacity to attain comprehension is itself comprehension.
– Abū Bakr aṣ-Ṣiddīq [CHI/PK438]

Sufi Aphorisms

The Unity of God is utterly inexpressible and indefinable.

– Abū Bakr ash-Shiblī [KAD/AJ70-71]

When the minds of the intelligent reach a high degree in professing Unity, they come to bewilderment.

– Abū'l-Qāsim al-Junayd [HAR/RS364]

Glory be to Him who assigned the creatures no path to His knowledge save the incapacity to know Him.

– Abū Naṣr as-Sarrāj [CHI/SD438]

Abū'l-'Abbās ad-Dīnawārī was asked, "By what means did you know God?" He replied, "By the fact that I do not know Him."

– Abū'l-'Abbās ad-Dīnawārī [ARB/SM63]

Sufi Poetry

Ponder on God's mercies,
But not on His essence.
For His works come forth from His essence,
Not His essence from His works.
His light shines on the whole universe,
Yet He Himself is hidden from the universe.

– Sa'd ud-Dīn Maḥmūd Shabistarī [LED/SR58]

Sufi Instruction

Tawḥīd is an idea (*ma'nā*) the definition of which cannot be defined, despite the vast and complete knowledge contained therein.

– Abū'l-Qāsim al-Junayd [KAD/AJ69]

The Shaikh [Abū'l-'Abbās] was asked regarding *Say He is God, the One* (112:1). He replied, "*Say* is an activity, *He* is an indication, and *God* is an expression. But the meaning of *tawḥīd* is beyond indication and expression."

– Abū'l-'Abbās Qaṣṣāb Āmulī [OKA/SG400]

The noblest saying referring to *tawḥīd* is the word of Abū Bakr: "Praise be to God, Who has vouchsafed to His creatures no other means of obtaining Knowledge of Him except through their impotence to attain Knowledge of Him."

– Abū'l-Qāsim al-Junayd [KAD/AJ68]

Whoever speaks of *tawḥīd* out of affectation is an idolater. Then what is it? No talk, no discussion, no equal, no likeness, no designation, no state. Only this: "He was always and always will be." The measure of *tawḥīd* is beyond the intellect; its reality is safe from the imagination.

– Abū Ya'qūb as-Sūsī [NUR/SM93]

Shiblī was asked, "Give us a pure affirmation of Unity with the language of a unique truth." "Woe to you!" he said. "Whoever answers about Unity with an explanation is a heretic. Whoever hints with allusions is a dualist. Whoever gestures to it is an idol-worshiper. If someone speaks about it he is unconscious, and if someone keeps silent about it he is ignorant. If someone imagines that he has reached it, he has not attained it. One sees it as near while it is far. The one who strives for ecstasy is destitute of it. Everything that you single out with your speculations and seize with your intellect in the most perfect of your ideas turns aside and comes back to you, a created phenomenon like yourselves."

– Abū Bakr ash-Shiblī [HAR/RS366-367]

The Only Worshipped

Foundational Sources

Your Lord has decreed that you worship none but Him.

– Qur'ān 17:23

Say [O Muḥammad]: "I am but a mortal like yourselves, but to whom it is revealed that your Lord is One God. So whoever hopes for the encounter with his Lord, let him work righteousness, and let him not associate anyone with Him in worship."

– Qur'ān 18:110

Verily I am God, there is no god but I; so worship Me!

– Qur'ān 20:14

We never sent a messenger before you, but that We revealed to him, saying, "there is no god but I, so worship Me!"

– Qur'ān 21:25

Your God is One God, so to Him surrender.

– Qur'ān 22:34

And set not up with God another god.
– Qur'ān 51:51

Someone asked 'Alī, "Did you come to know God intimately through Muḥammad or did you come to know Muḥammad through God?" He replied, "Had I come to know God through Muḥammad, I would not have served God, and Muḥammad would have been more firmly fixed in my soul than God. God acquainted me with Himself through Himself."
– 'Alī ibn Abī Ṭālib [REN/LS155-156]

Sufi Aphorisms

Sufism is looking in one direction and seeing One.
– Abū Sa'īd Ibn Abī'l-Khayr [JAM/UC33]

Tawḥīd is that nothing crosses your heart but God.
– Abū'l-'Abbas Sayyāri [NUR/SM92]

Unification (*tawḥīd*) is this: that nothing should occur to your mind except God.
– Abū'l-'Abbās Qāsim [NIC/RM157-158]

He who falls into the sea of *tawḥīd* grows thirstier day by day and can never drink his fill—for his thirst is quenched by God alone.
– Yūsuf ibn al-Ḥusayn [NUR/SM94]

Sufi Poetry

See but One, say but One, know but One,
In this are summed up the roots and branches of faith.
– Sa'd ud-Dīn Maḥmūd Shabistarī [NAS/SE51]

Whoever takes someone other than You as a substitute
is disappointed,
and whoever wants to stray away from You is lost.
– Ibn 'Aṭā' Allāh al-Iskandarī [DAN/BW125]

Be joyful with Him, not with "others":
He is spring, but others are like January.
Everything other than God is leading you astray,
be it your throne, kingdom, and crown.
– Jalāl ad-Dīn Rūmī [CHI/PL182-183]

Oh lover! Oh sincere one!
    If it is tidings you desire
Look upon the One who is in the city of existence;
    Pay no attention to any other.
Until you see wonders within yourself
    You must find the real goal.
In a deep sea you must dive
    There, where you cannot see the shore.
You must be one with the One . . .

– Meḥmed Muhyīddīn Üftāde [BAL/NG92]

I know nothing of two worlds—
All I know is the One—
    I seek only One,
    I know only One,
    I find only One,
And I sing of only One.
I am so drunk
On the wine of my Beloved
    that both worlds
Have slipped from my reach.
Now I have no business here
    but to reach
For the cup of my Beloved.

– Jalāl ad-Dīn Rūmī [STA/GB5]

You are the soul of my soul; without You I have no stability.
    If You are not in Paradise, by God! I do not esteem it.
If I look, my eyes see You; if I speak, You are my words.
    Other than observing You, I have nothing I want more.
Since I forgot myself, and thus went to You,
    whatever I say, whatever state I am in,
        I have no stability even for a moment.
If You should kill me seventy times, as they did Jerjis [Georges],[5]
    I would return and go to You because I have no shame.
Yūnus, also, is in love with You; show Your face to him.
    And You are my Beloved; I have no other beloved.

– Yūnus Emre [SMI/PY62]

[5] Jerjis was a prophet who came after Jesus; he was killed by his tribe seventy times and came back to life seventy times.

Sufi Instruction

The first station of one who attains and actualizes the science of *tawḥīd* is the freeing of his heart from thinking about things, that he might stand alone with God.

– Abū Sa'īd al-Kharrāz [NUR/SM95]

Tawḥīd is to turn away from the natural constitution, which is by its very nature blind to God's blessings and veiled to His Bounties. One cannot begin to turn toward God until one has turned away from the natural constitution.

– Abū 'Abd Allāh Ibn Khafīf [NUR/SM92-93]

Unification (*tawḥīd*) is the separation of the Eternal from that which was originated in Time, and departure from familiar haunts and separation from brethren and forgetfulness of what is known and unknown, and God only in place of All.

– Abū'l-Qāsim al-Junayd [KAD/AJ71]

When Ḥallāj was asked to define *tawḥīd*, he answered that it was to isolate the Eternal from the temporal. Ansāri commented, "Do you know wherein consists the *tawḥīd* of the Sufi? Negation of the temporal and affirmation of the Beginningless."

– Ḥusayn Ibn Manṣūr al-Ḥallāj [NUR/SM93]

The Shaikh [Abū Sa'īd] was asked: "What is Sufism?" He replied: "What we see as Sufism is polytheism." They said: "Oh Shaikh, why is that?" He answered: "Sufism consists of keeping the heart from the other or anything not He. But there is no other or anything not He."

– Abū Sa'īd Ibn Abī'l-Khayr [OKA/SG367]

If the love of the material or spiritual world is in any heart, there is no place for Divine Unity. Such hearts cannot discern gain and loss. In the heart, there is room for only one type of love, either of the worlds or of God. The two loves cannot come together in the arena of the heart.

– Abū Sa'īd Ibn Abī'l-Khayr [JAM/UC30]

He has missed the perfume of *tawḥīd* who conceptualizes it, witnesses realities, affirms Names, ascribes Attributes, and juggles with descriptions. He who affirms and denies all of these may have the properties and titles of one who professes Unity, but not his reality and existence.

– Abū Bakr ash-Shiblī [NUR/SM94]

"Asserting unity" (*tawḥīd*) is to make the heart one. In other words, it is to deliver and disengage it from attachment to what is other than the Real, both from the side of seeking and desire, and from the direction of knowledge and gnosis. In other words, seeking and desire are to be cut off from all objects of seeking and desire, and all objects of knowledge and intellect are to be eliminated from its insight's gaze. It turns its attentiveness away from every face, and no consciousness or awareness of other than the Real remains.

– 'Abd ar-Raḥmān Jāmī [MUR/CG151]

"Returning to the One" is for the heart to be in the One. It is cutting off and breaking away from attachment to external things, so that the self's seeking, loving, knowledge, and discernment are cut off and broken away from all that is sought after, all that is loved, all that is known, and all that is discerned. There will be only awareness of the Lord, and awareness of the Lord is non-awareness.[6]

– Liu Chih [MUR/CG151]

Independent

Foundational Sources

God is All-sufficient nor needs any being.

– Qur'ān 3:97

O men, you are the ones that have need of God; He is the All-sufficient, the All-laudable.

– Qur'ān 35:15

His is the Kingdom, and His is the praise, and He is powerful over everything.

– Qur'ān 64:1

Sufi Aphorisms

We and Thou are not separate from each other, but we need Thee, whereas Thou dost not need us.

– 'Abd ar-Raḥmān Jāmī [SCH/MD285]

[6] This passage is a gloss by the Chinese Muslim sage Liu Chih of the passage by the Persian Sufi master 'Abd ar-Raḥmān Jāmī immediately preceding it.

He was before every thing, and He shall endure after the passing away of every thing.

– 'Ayn al-Quḍāt Hamadhānī [ARB/SM83]

Sufi Instruction

You must not regard the eternal as a place of phenomena, or phenomena as a place of the eternal; and you must know that God is eternal and that you are phenomena, and that nothing of your genus is connected with Him, and that nothing of His Attributes is mingled in you, and that there is no homogeneity between the eternal and the phenomenal.

– Abū'l-Hasan 'Alī al-Hujwīrī [KAD/AJ71]

Know that there is not a divine Essence on the one hand; and, on the other, essences proper to creatures which are independent and subsist by themselves upon whom He has not conferred Being. There is nothing other than the divine Essence. It is this divine Essence which, without multiplying or dividing, is the essence of creatures; and, reciprocally, the essences of creatures are identical to the divine Essence. This does not mean that God has His essence and that creatures also have their own essences and that the divine Essence unites itself with them, or mixes with them, or infuses itself in them. All these things are impossible and that is not at all what I wish to say.

Rather, I mean that His essence, that is, His very being, through which creatures subsist and which rules them, is the essence of the creatures. In other words, when one speaks of the "essences of creatures" it is only a manner of expressing the manifestation of the true Being, when He clothes Himself in the properties which are implied by the predispositions of creatures; that is to say their immutable prototypes as they are in the divine science, non-existent, for ever and ever, being nothing but pure aspects or relationships in the heart of the divine Reality and having no being of their own.

– Amir 'Abd al-Qādir al-Jazā'irī [CHO/AK81]

The Source of All

Foundational Sources

Say: "Everything is from God."

– Qur'ān 4:78

Say: "God is the Creator of everything, and He is the One, the Omnipotent."

– Qur'ān 13:16

There is no thing whose treasuries are not with Us, and We only send it down but in a known measure.

– Qur'ān 15:21

We did not create the heavens and the earth, and all that is between them, save through the Real.

– Qur'ān 15:85

He created the heavens and the earth through the Real (*al-Ḥaqq*).

– Qur'ān 16:3

God did not create the heavens, the earth, and what is between them, save through the Real and in an appointed term.

– Qur'ān 30:8

We did not create the heavens and the earth and all that is between them in play; We did not create them save through the Real, but most of them do not know.

– Qur'ān 44:38-39

I was a Treasure but was not known, so I loved to be known; I created the creatures and made Myself known to them, so they came to know Me.

– *Ḥadīth Qudsī* [CHI/SD437]

Sufi Aphorisms

Nothing proceeds from the One but one.

– Ibn Sīnā (Avicenna) [CHI/SD439]

Sufi Poetry

Nothing comes to You from anyone;
    nothing comes from You to anyone;
everything comes from You to You,
    You are everything, and that is all.

– Khwāja 'Abd Allāh Anṣārī [ADD/VN79]

David said to the manifesting God,
“O Thou who art free of poverty and need,
What is the wisdom of creating the creatures?
This is a mystery no creature understands.”
God said, “I was a treasure, full of jewels,
hidden from the discerning eye of every jeweler.
I Myself saw in Myself all those jewels
without the intermediary of any locus of manifestation.
I wanted to take all those hidden jewels
and show them outside My own Essence,
So that outside this sitting place of mystery
their properties may become distinguished.
All may thereby find a route to existence,
all may become aware of self and other.
I created a few discerning jewelers
so that they might uncover those jewels
And make manifest the jewel of beauty,
that the bazaar of love might become busy.
With it they will adorn the faces of the beautiful
and increase the love of the lovers.”
The names, hidden in the Essence, could be seen
only through the manifestation of the things.
The names had a hidden beauty,
but they rested in the levels of possibility.
With one unveiled glance, that hidden Beauty
became manifest in the loci of possibility.
Every auspicious beauty and perfection
scattered throughout the cosmos—
Consider it a ray of that perfection and beauty,
a differentiation of the level of undifferentiation.
See, for example, the attribute of knowledge,
disclosing itself in the loci of the scholars:
It is the knowledge of God that has appeared
but within the levels of delimitation.

– ‘Abd ar-Raḥmān Jāmī [MUR/TI62]

The End of All

Foundational Sources

Say: “Surely we belong to God, and to Him we return.”
– Qur’ān 2:156

To God belongs the Unseen in the heavens and the earth. To Him the whole matter shall be returned; so serve Him, and put your trust in Him. Your Lord is not heedless of the things you do.

– Qur'ān 11:123

Every soul shall taste death; and We test you with evil and with good as a trial, and to Us you shall be returned.

– Qur'ān 21:35

And He is God; there is no god but He . . . and unto Him you shall be returned.

– Qur'ān 28:70

Sufi Aphorisms

Everything returns to its root.

– 'Azīz ad-Dīn Nasafī [MUR/TI379]

Sufi Instruction

The final goal of the soul's existence is the abode of holiness and the world of the afterworld. The final goal of her intention, toward which she turns by essence with respect to innate disposition, is gnosis and arrival at the encounter with God. Once the knowledge of *tawḥīd* becomes plain for someone and he understands the guideposts of the Lordship, within which the first origins and the furthest final ends are investigated, he will know for certain that each thing's origin is the same as its final goal. So, the origin of the fully knowing soul is from God, and her end point is to God. *Their call therein is,* "*Glory to Thee, O God,*" *and their greeting,* "*Peace,*" *and the last of their call is,* "*Praise belongs to God, Lord of the worlds*" (10:10).

– Ṣadr ad-Dīn Muḥammad Shīrāzī [CHI/EG87]

The Perishing of All Otherness

Foundational Sources

And say: "The Real has come and the unreal has vanished away; surely the unreal is ever certain to vanish."

– Qur'ān 17:81

And call not upon another god with God; there is no god but He. Everything is perishing except His Face. His is the Judgment, and unto

Him you shall be returned.

– Qur'ān 28:88

All that dwells upon the earth is perishing, yet still abides the Face of your Lord, majestic, splendid.

– Qur'ān 55:26

When I [God] love him, I am his hearing through which he hears, his eyesight through which he sees, his hand through which he holds, and his foot through which he walks.

– *Ḥadīth Qudsī* [CHI/SD441]

The truest verse sung by the Arabs is the line of Labīd,
"Is not everything other than God unreal?"

– *Ḥadīth* [CHI/PK439]

Sufi Aphorisms

The end of *tawḥīd* is to forget other than *tawḥīd* through *tawḥīd.*

– Abū Bakr ash-Shiblī [NUR/SM95]

Oneness (*tawḥīd*) is the subsistence of God through the annihilation of everything other than He.

– Abū Bakr ash-Shiblī [NUR/SM95]

Tawḥīd is to take leave of the constrictions of formal limitations and to arrive at the spaciousness of annihilation in Eternity.

– Abū'l-Qāsim al-Junayd [NUR/SM95]

There is no creature in *tawḥīd*; no one finds God but God. *Tawḥīd* is God's alone; creatures are but uninvited guests.

– Abū Bakr ash-Shiblī [NUR/SM95]

Tawḥīd is the obliteration of the traces of human nature and the naked presence of the Divinity.

– Ruwaym ibn Aḥmad [NUR/SM95]

Tawḥīd is that one is annihilated in devotion to God and removed from all self-will, and that one habituates the tongue to truth and restrains the heart from all relationships with "other than God," considering it as obliterated.

– Darvish Muḥammad Tabasī [NUR/SM94]

Sufi Poetry

Before the Infinite,
all that is finite is nothingness:
Everything is passing away,
except the Face of God (28:88).
– Jalāl ad-Dīn Rūmī [HEL/RD188]

Lover, beloved, and love—
all the three are one.
When union comes in,
what has separation to do?
– Fakhr ad-Dīn ʻIrāqī [SCH/TV70]

When you lose yourself in God,
you proclaim the divine Unity.
Lose the sense of "being lost"—
that is complete detachment!
– Sharaf ad-Dīn Manīrī [JAC/HL14]

When my Beloved appears,
With what eye do I see Him?
With His eye, not with mine,
For none sees Him except Himself.
– Muḥyī ad-Dīn Ibn al-ʻArabī [SCH/TV38]

What is this *tawḥīd*, this learning God's Unity?
Burning oneself to ashes before the One!
But when my pen attempts to describe this state
The pen is shattered and the paper torn to shreds.
– Jalāl ad-Dīn Rūmī [NUR/SM72]

All is in Me; there is none other than I.
I am the being that became when He said, "Be."[7]
I am the life and the only living.
I am the love, the lover, and the beloved.
In human shape is all and everything.
In the shape of His mercy He made Me.
– Badr ad-Dīn as-Simawnī [BAY/PB13]

[7] A common Qur'ānic description of the immediacy of the Divine creative power: "And when He decrees a thing, He but says to it 'Be,' and it is" (2:117). The same expression also appears in verses 3:47, 6:73, 16:40, 19:35, 36:82, and 40:68.

In the market, in the cloister—only God I saw.
In the valley and on the mountain—only God I saw.
Him I have seen beside me oft in tribulation;
In favor and in fortune—only God I saw.
In prayer and fasting, in praise and contemplation,
In the religion of the Prophet—only God I saw.
Neither soul nor body, accident nor substance,
Qualities nor causes—only God I saw.
I oped mine eyes and by the light of His face around me
In all the eye discovered—only God I saw.
Like a candle I was melting in His fire:
Amidst the flames outflashing—only God I saw.
Myself with mine own eyes I saw most clearly,
But when I looked with God's eyes—only God I saw.
I passed away into nothingness, I vanished,
And lo, I was the All-living—only God I saw.

– Bābā Kūhī Shīrāzī [NIC/MI59]

Sufi Instruction

None grasps Him save He Himself. None knows Him but He Himself. . . . He knows Himself by Himself. . . . Other-than-He cannot grasp Him. His impenetrable veil is His own Oneness. Other-than-He does not cloak Him. His veil is His very existence. He is veiled by His Oneness in a manner that cannot be explained. Other-than-He does not see Him; whether prophet, envoy, or perfected saint, or angel near unto Him. His prophet is He Himself. His envoy is He. His message is He. His word is He. He has sent word of His Ipseity by Himself, from Himself to Himself, without intermediary or causality other than Himself. . . . Other-than-He has no existence and so cannot bring itself to naught.

– Muḥyī ad-Dīn Ibn al-'Arabī [BUR/SD17-18]

IV. Concentration upon Unity: The Manifold Aspects of *Dhikrullāh*

Objective Tawḥīd: No existence but God

	Divine Initiative		
Microcosmic Pole	God's Remembrance of Man[*] *Divine preliminary* The Command to Remembrance[◊] *Divine injunction* Perpetual Remembrance[+] *dominating activity*	[IDENTICAL SUPERSCRIPTS INDICATE COMPLEMENTARY CATEGORIES] The "Signs" as Reminder[†] *cosmic initiative* The Qur'ān as Reminder[‡] *revelatory initiative*	*Macrocosmic Pole*
Inception	The Polish of the Heart *purification* → The Passing from All but the Remembered *the dhikr alone* →	The Passing from the Remembrance *the dhikr as veil* → The Passing Away of the Rememberer *entry to tawḥīd*	*Perfection*
Microcosmic Pole	Man's Remembrance of God[*] *human evocation* The Necessity of Remembrance[◊] *human need* The Significance of Remembrance[+] *supreme activity*	Universal Remembrance[†] *cosmic evocation* The People of Remembrance[‡] *example / reminding* The People of Heedlessness[‡] *warning / forgetting*	*Macrocosmic Pole*
	Created Response		

Subjective Tawḥīd: No self but God

IV. Concentration upon Unity: The Practice of *Dhikrullāh*

Overview: *Dhikrullāh*

The inculcation of *tawḥīd* requires a methodic application that is both an extension and essentialization of the ordinary rites of the religion. This repetitive recitation (*dhikr*) of the Divine Name, or other sacred utterance, is at once a remembrance, recollection, mention, and evocation. It is, most fundamentally, a means of making the heart present to God and God present to the heart. The remembrance of the Name is so fundamental that it forms, in some variation, a central spiritual method in nearly every sacred tradition. Islam is, in this respect, no exception.

Just as the cosmological pairing of the microcosm and the macrocosm—distinguishing between the human subject and the creation as a whole—proved of relevance in elucidating the subtleties of *tawḥīd*, so also is this fundamental pairing relevant in the context of *dhikr*. Further, as *dhikr* possesses a specifically dynamic aspect, it is also important to distinguish between the activity of God and that of the created order. In a sense, as informed by the doctrine of *tawḥīd*, every activity goes back to God; but from the perspective of existence itself, we may also speak of a Divine initiative and created response.

In the context of the human microcosm, God's remembrance of man is a necessary preliminary to man's remembrance of God, for God remembers us and only in light of this may we be said to remember Him. Further, the Divine injunction to remembrance, as given in the Qur'ān, is paralleled by the human need for remembrance. This is further intensified in light of the injunction to remember abundantly, which is indicative of the profound significance of remembrance for man. There is the sense—reflected in the tradition—that human beings must initially be led to remembrance, but that following a certain spiritual maturation, remembrance becomes the most precious nourishment and balm.

In the context of the larger macrocosm, the tradition speaks of two "books," that of the Qur'ān and that of creation. In both of these books, God reveals His "signs" (*āyāt*): in the case of the Qur'ān these are the words and sentences of the revealed book, while in the case of the creation itself, these are the aspects of the created order that bear particular witness to the Divine reality. The Qur'ān itself is first and foremost a reminder to humanity, as the text itself makes clear. The human response to this reminder is broadly twofold—remembrance or heedlessness. The tradition recognizes that the creation itself not only yields signs for human remembrance, but is itself, by virtue of its nature and origin, in a state of remembrance and glorification of God.

Finally, we may speak of four stages in the perfection of remembrance: the initial purification or polishing of the heart; then the experience of the passing from awareness of all but the remembered, the *dhikr* alone persisting; at a further level of subtlety, the *dhikr* itself becomes a veil and the act of remembrance itself must pass from the awareness of the invoker; at the final stage, the rememberer himself passes away and in this, the state of *fanā'*, the reality of *tawḥīd* is unveiled. At each successive stage, a more subtle and intimate covering over the Divine Reality is removed, until only God remains.

God's Remembrance of Man

Foundational Sources

And when My servants question you concerning Me—surely I am near. I answer the prayer of the suppliant when he prays to Me.

– Qur'ān 2:186

I am the sitting companion of him who remembers Me.

– *Ḥadīth Qudsī* [CHI/SD436]

Sufi Aphorisms

I call to You. . . . No, it is You who calls me to Yourself. How could I say, "It is You!" if you had not said to me, "It is I?"

– Ḥusayn Ibn Manṣūr al-Ḥallāj [MAS/3P42]

Not a day passes but that the Exalted cries out, "O my servant, you treat Me unjustly. I remember you, but You forget Me. I invite you to Myself, but you go to others."

– Sahl al-Tustarī [SCH/PS211]

Remembrance entails continuous presence and the vision of the One remembered. Do not forget to remember the One who never forgets to remember you and do not forget to thank the One who never forgets your devotion.

– Abū Madyan [COR/AM132]

Moses said, "My Lord, art Thou far that I should call out to Thee, or art Thou near that I should whisper to Thee?" God replied, "I am the sitting companion of him who remembers Me, so I am with him." Moses said, "Which act is most beloved to Thee, My Lord?" He said, "You should remember Me much in every state."

– Khwāja 'Abdallāh Anṣārī [CHI/SD436]

Sufi Poetry

"If I hate my sins, will God love me?"
"No—
But if He remembers you,
Then you will remember Him—
So stand in wait."

– Rābi'a al-'Adawīya [UPT/DH40]

You are the Invoker prior to invokers,
You are the Origin of benevolence prior to servants turning to You,
You are the Munificent in giving prior to the asking of seekers,
and You are the Giver who,
in respect to what You have given us,
asks us for a loan!

– Ibn 'Aṭā' Allāh al-Iskandarī [DAN/BW126]

Your call "O God!" is My call "I am here."
Your supplication is My message, dear,
And all your striving to come close to Me
Is but a sign that *I* draw you to Me.
Your loving quest and pain: signs of My grace!
In each "O God!" a hundred "Here's My Face!"

– Jalāl ad-Dīn Rūmī [SCH/IW170]

Sufi Instruction

The Shaikh [Abū Sa'īd] was questioned about the meaning of this Qur'ānic verse: *Verily, God's remembrance is greater* (29:45). He replied: "The meaning is that God's remembrance of His servant is greater. This is so because the servant cannot recall Him, until He first recalls the servant. It is indeed greater that the Lord remembers the servant and gives him divine assistance, so that the servant as well may remember the Lord. If you look at this carefully, it is God Who is remembering Himself. The servant does not exist in the matter at all."

– Abū Sa'īd Ibn Abī'l-Khayr [OKA/SG459-60]

The believer is he who knows that behind this wall there is Someone who is aware of every single one of our states. He sees us, even if we do not see Him. For the believer this has become a certainty. In contrast another person says, "No, this is only a tale," and has no faith. The day is coming when God will box his ears and he will be sorry. He will say, "Alas! I said an evil thing! I was wrong! It was indeed all He, but I denied Him!"

For instance, you are playing the rebeck and know that I am behind the wall. For certain you will keep on playing. You will not stop, for you are a rebeck-player. After all, the purpose of this ritual prayer is not that you should stand and bow and prostrate yourself all day long. Its purpose is that you should possess continuously that spiritual state which appears to you in prayer: Whether asleep or awake, writing or reading, in all your states you should never be empty of the remembrance of God; rather, you should be one of *those who are constantly at their prayers* (70:23).

– Jalāl ad-Dīn Rūmī [CHI/PL153]

Man's Remembrance of God

Foundational Sources

So remember Me, and I will remember you; and be thankful to Me; and do not be ungrateful towards Me.

– Qur'ān 2:152

They have forgotten God, so He has forgotten them.

– Qur'ān 9:67

Your Lord has said, "Call upon Me and I will answer you."

– Qur'ān 40:60

I am present in My servant's thought of Me, and I am with him when he remembers Me. If he mentions Me in his self, I mention him in My Self, and if he mentions Me in an assembly, I mention him in a better assembly than that.[1] If he approaches Me by a hand's breadth, I draw near to him by an arm's length; and if he draws near to Me by an arm's length, I draw near to him by a fathom. If he comes to Me walking, I come to him running.

– *Ḥadīth Qudsī* [HIR/DS46]

Sufi Aphorisms

I have read in some of the revealed books that the Real most high has given two things to the community of Muḥammad that He gave to neither the angel Gabriel nor the angel Michael. One is *Remember me; I will remember you* (2:152) and the second is *Call me; I will answer you* (40:60).

– Mālik ibn Dīnār [LOS/AM89]

Sufi Poetry

Let's say the name of God all the time.
Let's see what my Lord does.
Let's travel the Way always.
Let's see what my Lord does.

Just when you least expect it,
suddenly the veil is lifted.
The remedy arrives in time.
Let's see what my Lord does.

What did Yūnus do?
What did he do?
He found a straight Path,
held the hand of a guide.
Let's see what my Lord does.

– Yūnus Emre [HEL/DS22]

Sufi Instruction

God has said: "When My servant becomes altogether occupied with Me, then I make his happiness consist in the remembrance of Myself, and when I have made his happiness and his delight consist in that remembrance, he desires Me and I desire him, and when he desires Me

[1] The "better assembly" is typically understood by the Islamic tradition to refer to the assembly of angels around the Divine Throne.

and I desire him, I raise the veils between Me and him and I become manifest before his eyes. These do not forget Me, when others forget."

– Ḥasan al-Baṣrī [SMI/RM1]

Know—and may God be merciful to you—that the disciple (*faqīr*), when he exchanges the remembrance of all things for the remembrance (*dhikr*) of God, purifies his servitude, and whosoever serves God in a pure and unmixed way is holy. So remember only God; be God's alone; for if you are God's, God will be yours and blessed is he who belongs to God so that God is his. Let the mention of God's word *Remember Me and I will remember you* (2:152) suffice to prove the excellence of the remembrance (*dhikr*) of God. And the word which the Prophet spoke on behalf of his Lord: *I am the Companion of him who calls upon Me* (*ḥadīth qudsī*).

– Mulay al-'Arabī ad-Darqāwī [BUR/LS2]

As long as you do not look for something, you do not find it. However, the Beloved is an exception—before you find Him you do not look for Him. Man desires something that he has not found, he looks for it day and night, but it would be amazing if his search continued after he had found the object of his desire. A desire fixed on an object already found is not of the human spirit. Man cannot imagine such a desire because he is always attracted by novelty. The search which concerns something already found is proper to God, for God Almighty has everything in His power. "The one who finds is the Magnanimous," for the One who finds is the One who has found everything. *Be, and it is* (*kun fayakūn*) (6:73). The Almighty God is the Seeker for "it is He who is the Seeker and the Dominator." That is the meaning of this saying: "Oh man, as long as you remain in this ephemeral search, you are far from the goal. When your search is annihilated in the search for God and when the search coming from God is greater than yours, then you become a real seeker because of the search of God."

– Jalāl ad-Dīn Rūmī [VIT/RS145]

The Command to Remembrance

Foundational Sources

Remember He who gave you guidance, although before you were gone astray.

– Qur'ān 2:198

Call upon your Lord in humility and in secret.
– Qur'ān 7:55

In the Messenger of God you have a good example for whosoever hopes for God and the Last Day, and remembers God often.
– Qur'ān 33:21

Men and women who have surrendered, believing men and believing women, obedient men and obedient women, truthful men and truthful women, enduring men and enduring women, humble men and humble women, men and women who give in charity, men who fast and women who fast, men and women who guard their private parts, men and women who remember God abundantly—for them God has prepared forgiveness and a vast reward.
– Qur'ān 33:35

O you who believe! Remember God abundantly; and glorify Him morning and evening.
– Qur'ān 33:41

Is it not time that the hearts of those who believe should be humbled to the remembrance of God and the Truth which He has sent down, and that they should not be as those to whom the Book was given aforetime, and the term seemed overlong to them, so that their hearts became hard, and many of them are ungodly?
– Qur'ān 57:16

O believers, when proclamation is made for prayer on the Day of Congregation, hasten to the remembrance of God and leave trading aside; that is better for you, if you but knew. Then, when the prayer is finished, disperse in the land and seek God's bounty, and remember God frequently, that you may prosper.
– Qur'ān 62:9-10

O child of Adam, when you remember Me you are grateful to Me, and when you forget Me you are unfaithful to Me.
– *Ḥadīth Qudsī* [HIR/DS32]

Let your tongue be moistened with the invocation of God morning and evening, and then no fault will fall upon you.
– *Ḥadīth* [NAK/IS7]

A man said: "O Messenger of God, the revealed laws of faith have become too many for me, so tell me of one thing to hold fast to." He said: "Let your tongue never cease to be moist from the remembrance of God the Almighty."

– *Ḥadīth* [TAY/GW74]

He who sits down without remembering God the Almighty has committed an omission which God will hold against him, and he who lies down without remembering God the Almighty has committed an omission which God will hold against him.

– *Ḥadīth* [TAY/GW76]

Sufi Poetry

What is sweeter than the remembrance of the Friend?
Hey, do not sit idle like this! Invoke!

– Jalāl ad-Dīn Rūmī [CHI/PL159]

Stop talking!
What a shame you have no familiarity
with inner silence!
Polish your heart for a day or two:
make that mirror your book of contemplation.

– Jalāl ad-Dīn Rūmī [HEL/JR148]

Your intelligence is spread over a hundred "important" affairs,
over thousands of desires and concerns great and small.
You must unite the scattered parts by means of love,
so that you may become as sweet as Damascus and Samarkand.
When you have become united,
particle by particle, from out of perplexity,
then it is possible to stamp the King's seal upon you.

– Jalāl ad-Dīn Rūmī [HEL/JR83]

My God,
were it not incumbent to accept Your command,
I would declare You far too exalted for me to remember You,
for I remember You in my measure, not in Your measure,
and my scope can hardly reach the point
where I may be a locus for calling You holy!
Among Your greatest favors to us
is the running of Your remembrance across our tongues
and Your permission to us to supplicate You,

declare You exalted, and call You holy!
My God,
inspire us with Your remembrance alone and in assemblies,
by night and day, publicly and secretly,
in prosperity and adversity!
Make us intimate with silent remembrance,
employ us in purified works and effort pleasing to You,
and reward us with the full balance!
My God,
love-mad hearts are enraptured by You,
disparate intellects are brought together by knowing You,
hearts find no serenity except in remembering You,
souls find no rest except in seeing You.

– Zayn al-'Abidīn 'Alī ibn al-Ḥusayn [CHI/PI255-256]

Sufi Instruction

All good lies in the remembrance (*dhikr*) of God, since He said: *For men and women who remember God often, God has prepared forgiveness and a great reward* (33:35). He also said: *Remember Me and I will remember you* (2:152) and, *Give thanks to Me and be not unbelievers* (2:152). Likewise: *Woe unto them whose hearts are hardened against the mention* (*dhikr*) *of God; those are in manifest error* (39:22). The Prophet made known to us these divine words: *I am near to him who calls upon Me* (*ḥadīth qudsī*).

Let that suffice to show the excellence of remembrance and the fault in forgetfulness. And if the divine words we have quoted were not enough for us, then nothing would be enough and there would be no good in us. God promises an immense reward to those who remember and indeed we have no need of anything other than that. All we need is to go against our passionate desires, for by that we acquire intuitive knowledge, which in turn gives us the great certainty, and the great certainty will deliver us from all doubts and cares and will lead us towards the presence of the infinitely knowing King. There is no divinity but He.

– Mulay al-'Arabī ad-Darqāwī [BUR/LS28]

The Necessity of Remembrance

Sufi Aphorisms

The breath that does not repeat the name of God is a wasted breath.

– Kabīr [VAU/TP63]

Remembrance of the mighty and glorious Lord is food for my soul, praising Him is wine for my soul, and shame before Him is clothing for my soul.

– Dhul-Nūn al-Miṣrī [LOS/AM180]

Sufi Poetry

Separation from Him is a well, remembrance of Him a rope:
At the bottom of the well a Joseph clings to the rope.

– Jalāl ad-Dīn Rūmī [CHI/PL159]

Drink the potion of His remembrance
  and be delivered from thoughts!
If you were not to enter into all this strife,
  oh man pleasing to God, how would you lose?

– Jalāl ad-Dīn Rūmī [CHI/PL159]

Today I forgot my ritual prayer due to my excessive love,
And I do not know whether it's morning or evening;
For Your recollection, O Lord, is my food and my drink,
And Your face, if I see it, is the cure of my ailment.

– Jalāl ad-Dīn Rūmī [SCH/TV29]

If you're serious about joining
  the people of vision
you must move from speech
  to the inner state.
You won't become one
  just by chanting "Unity"—
Repeating the word *sugar*
  won't make your mouth sweet.

– Dārā Shikūh [FID/LA125]

My tears would flood the Oxus River
  if my eyes didn't forever behold Your Vision, Friend.
Driven insane with the pain of separation,
  my heart would sink in its own blood
    if it did not float in the river of Your Remembrance.
I would devise a thousand tricks to spring my soul
  out of the cage of this body,
if it did not insist on enduring this exile,
  to arrive in obedience at her wedding with You, Beloved.

– Abū Sa'īd Ibn Abī'l-Khayr [ABR/NS34]

Your hope in my heart is the rarest treasure.
Your Name on my tongue is the sweetest word.
My choicest hours
Are the hours I spend with You—

O God, I can't live in this world
Without remembering You—
How can I endure the next world
Without seeing Your face?

I am a stranger in Your country
And lonely among Your worshippers:
This is the substance of my complaint.

– Rābiʿa al-ʿAdawīya [UPT/DH44]

Sufi Instruction

What really counts on the path of God the Exalted, having obeyed commands and avoided forbidden things, is to persevere in remembering God; so keep to it, O disciple, in all situations, with heart and tongue, at all times and places.

– ʿAbdallah Ibn ʿAlawi al-Ḥaddād [BAD/MR59]

Lastly, my brother, I strongly advise you—"religion is sincere counsel" (*ḥadīth*)—not to give up the remembrance (*dhikr*) of your Lord, as He Himself told you to do it, *standing, sitting and reclining* (4:104) and in all conditions, for we need nothing but that, we, you and every man, whoever he may be. Listen to what I am about to say to you and do not forget it, do not take it lightly or let it go unheeded: in the course of the past fifty-five years or so, I have said to many a brother: every single man has any number of needs, but in reality all men need only one thing, which is truly to practice the remembrance of God; if they have acquired that, they will not want for anything, whether they possess it or do not possess it.

– Mulay al-ʿArabī ad-Darqāwī [BUR/LS37]

Perpetual Remembrance

Foundational Sources

Remember your Lord in abundance, and praise Him in the evening and in the morning.

– Qur'ān 3:41

When you have performed the prayer, remember God standing, sitting, and reclining.

– Qur'ān 4:103

And remember your Lord within yourself, in humility and awe, with subdued voice, at morning and evening. And do not be among the heedless.

– Qur'ān 7:205

In houses which God has allowed to be raised up, wherein His name is remembered; in them He is glorified morning and evening by men whom neither commerce nor trafficking diverts from the remembrance of God, the observance of prayer, or paying of alms, fearing a day when hearts and eyes shall be overturned, that God may reward them for the best of what they did and increase them of His favor.

– Qur'ān 24:36-38

Yet those who are with your Lord do glorify Him by night and day, and are never wearied.

– Qur'ān 41:38

And remember the Name of your Lord morning and evening; bow down before Him a portion of the night, and glorify Him through the long night.

– Qur'ān 76:25

He [Muḥammad] was remembering God all the while.

– 'Ā'isha [CHI/SD435]

God, Almighty and Exalted, put a limit on all the obligations that He ordered human beings except for *dhikr*. For it there is no limit.

– 'Abd Allāh Ibn 'Abbās [KAB/CI48]

Certainly, God, the Glorified, the Sublime, has made His remembrance the light for hearts which hear with its help despite deafness, see with its help despite blindness, and become submissive with its help despite unruliness. . . . There are some people devoted to the remembrance of God who have adopted it in place of worldly matters so that commerce or trade does not turn them away from it. They pass their life in it.

– 'Alī ibn Abī Ṭālib [ALI/NB440-441]

Sufi Aphorisms

How happy are those who are always praying.

– Muḥammad Shams ad-Dīn Ḥāfiẓ [NAS/SE49]

Keep God, the Beloved, always in your heart. Let your prayer, *dhikr*, be the prayer of your heart.

– ʻAbd al-Khāliq Ghijduwānī [VAU/TP70]

I make abundant remembrance of You not because I have forgotten You; that is simply what flows from the tongue.

– Dhul-Nūn al-Miṣrī [VAU/TP72]

Once, a person approached such a saint with this request: "When you are beseeching God, if memory of me comes to mind, please offer a prayer on my behalf." Replied that dervish: "Woe to that time when memory of you comes to mind!"

– Niẓām ad-Dīn Awliyā' [LAW/MH320]

Sufi Poetry

Engage yourself as much as you can, my friend,
in remembrance of God;
if you can work, remember Him at your labor.
Be pure, take not one breath without ablution;
for your companions, seek none but the Pure.

– Shāh Niʻmatullāh Walī [POU/KL199]

The ritual prayer is five times daily,
but the guide for lovers is the verse,
they who are in prayer continually (70:43).
The headache of intoxication in those heads
isn't relieved by five times, nor by five hundred thousand.
"Visit once a week" is not the ration for lovers;
the soul of sincere lovers has an intense craving to drink.
"Visit once a week" is not the ration for those fish,
since they feel no spiritual joy without the Sea.

– Jalāl ad-Dīn Rūmī [HEL/JR165]

Sufi Instruction

Remembrance is that by means of which man preserves that knowledge which he has attained, so it is akin to memory except that memory is spoken of in respect of its function of acquisition, whereas remembrance is spoken of in respect of its function of "rendering present". Remembrance is also used to refer to the presence of a thing either in one's heart or in one's speech. Thus, it is said that there are two types of remembrance: remembrance of the heart and remembrance of the tongue, and each comprises two further kinds of remembrance: a remembrance which follows forgetfulness, and a remembrance which does not follow forgetfulness but which on the contrary expresses a continuous remembering.

– al-Rāghib al-Iṣfahānī [KAZ/OL14]

The Significance of Remembrance

Foundational Sources

Recite that which has been revealed to you of the Book, and perform the prayer; prayer preserves from indecency and dishonor; but the remembrance of God is greater.

– Qur'ān 29:45

Indeed God has angels who roam the roads, seeking out the people of Invocation (*dhikr*). When they find a group invoking God, they call out: "Come hither to what you have been looking for!" And they surround them with their wings, reaching up to the lowest heaven. Their Lord questions them (yet He knows better than they): "What do My servants say?" They reply: "They glorify and magnify You; they praise You and repeat Your praises." He asks: "Have they seen Me?" They reply: "No, by God, they have not seen You." Then He asks: "And how would it be if they were to see Me?" They reply: "If they were to see You, they would be stronger in service to You, stronger in repeating Your praises, and more profuse in glorifying You." He asks: "What do they ask of Me?" They reply: "They ask You for Paradise." He asks: "And have they seen it?" They reply: "No, O Lord, by God, they have not seen it." Then He asks: "And how would it be if they were to see it?" They reply: "If they were to see it, they would be stronger in striving for it, stronger in seeking it, and greater in their desire for it." He asks: "Then from what do they seek refuge?" They reply: "From the Fire." He asks: "And have they seen it?" They reply: "No, O Lord, by God, they have not seen it." Then He asks: "And how would it be if they were to see it?" They reply: "They would be faster in their flight from it and greater in their fear of it." He says: "I call you all to witness that I have forgiven them." But one angel will say: "Among them is so-and-so who is not one of them, for he only came out of need." God will reply: "They are the sitting-companions. No-one who sits with them can be unhappy."

– *Ḥadīth Qudsī* [HIR/DS81-82]

The one who mentions or remembers God among those who forget Him is like a light inside a dark house.

– *Ḥadīth* [KAB/GB143]

The one who mentions or remembers God among those who forget Him is like a green tree in the midst of dry ones.

– *Ḥadīth* [KAB/GB143]

The one who mentions or remembers God among those who forget Him is like the fighter amidst those who run away.

– *Ḥadīth* [KAB/GB143]

The likeness of him who remembers his Lord to him who does not remember his Lord is as the likeness of the living to the dead.

– *Ḥadīth* [TAY/GW74]

The world and everything in it is cursed, except for *dhikr* and what attends *dhikr*, and the teacher, and the student.

– *Ḥadīth* [KAB/GB97]

On being asked, "Which act is most meritorious?" the Messenger of God said, "That you die while your tongue is moistened with the invocation of God."

– *Ḥadīth* [NAK/IS7]

The Messenger of God has said: "When you pass the gardens of Paradise enjoy their fruits." They asked, "And what are the gardens of Paradise?" He said, "The gatherings of remembrance (*dhikr*)."

– *Ḥadīth* [FRI/SS134]

The Prophet was asked, "Which of the servants of God is best in rank before God on the Day of Resurrection?" He said, "The ones who remember Him much." I said, "O Messenger of God, what about the fighter in the way of God?" He answered, ". . . truly those who do *dhikr* are better than him in rank."

– *Ḥadīth* [KAB/GB99]

The Prophet once asked his companions, "Shall I tell you about the best of all deeds, the best act of piety in the eyes of your Lord, which will elevate your status in the Hereafter, and carries more virtue than the spending of gold and silver in the service of God and meeting your enemy and slaying or being slain in the path of God?" They said, "Yes, O Messenger of God." He said, "The constant remembrance of God."

– *Ḥadīth* [KAB/GB99]

Sufi Aphorisms

Do not grieve over the goal while remembrance of the One adored exists.

– Dhul-Nūn al-Miṣrī [LOS/AM184]

The sum total of our life is a breath spent in the company of the Beloved.

– Abū Sa'īd Ibn Abī'l-Khayr [ABR/NS10]

Every breath containing the recollection of God is conjoined with the Throne.

– Sulaymān ibn 'Abd Allāh [ARB/SM57]

One cannot taste the intimacy of remembrance without having suffered the desolation of forgetfulness.

– Abū 'Uthmān al-Hīrī [SCH/PS212]

The exterior of invocation would not exist were it not for the interior of contemplation and meditation.

– Ibn 'Aṭā' Allāh al-Iskandarī [DAN/BW110]

There is a punishment for every created thing; for the mystic, it is being disconnected from the remembrance of God.

– Dhul-Nūn al-Miṣrī [REN/KG291]

Do not say, "I am nothing." Neither say, "I am something." Do not say, "I need such and such a thing" nor yet, "I need nothing." But say, "Allāh," and you will see marvels.

– Mulay al-'Arabī ad-Darqāwī [KAB/CI49]

Someone saw Junayd carrying a rosary and said to him, "In spite of your eminence you still ply the beads?" He replied, "I do not stray from a path that has led me to my Lord."

– Abū'l-Qāsim al-Junayd [REN/LS129]

Remembrance is a charter of God's Friendship. Whosoever has been granted the grace of remembrance has been given the following injunction, "You are really the friend of God."

– Abū 'Alī Daqqāq [VAL/CD35-36]

Dhikr is the medicine of the sinners, the familiarity of the estranged, the treasure of those who practice reliance, the repast of those who possess certitude, the adornment of those who are connected, the starting-point of knowers, the carpet of those brought near Him, and the intoxicant of lovers.

– Abū Sa'īd Aḥmad al-Kharrāz [KAB/GB144]

Sufi Poetry

Remembrance makes people desire the journey;
it makes them into travelers.

– Jalāl ad-Dīn Rūmī [CHI/PL159]

In the outside world, wind sets a tree in motion.
In the inside, remembrance rustles the leaves of the heart's tree.

– Jalāl ad-Dīn Rūmī [CHI/PL159]

If your thought is frozen, practice remembrance of God.
Recollection of God brings thought into movement:
make remembrance the sun for this congealed thought.

– Jalāl ad-Dīn Rūmī [HEL/JR153]

O God,
Another Night is passing away,
Another Day is rising—
Tell me that I have spent the Night well so I can be at peace,
Or that I have wasted it, so I can mourn for what is lost.
I swear that ever since the first day You brought me back to life,
The day You became my Friend,
I have not slept—
And even if You drive me from your door,
I swear again that we will never be separated—
Because You are alive in my heart.

– Rābi'a al-'Adawīya [UPT/DH51]

Dhikr is the source of all good things.
So reckless was I, so much time did I waste.

Those days are forever gone; what to do now?
Let us, from now on, take advantage of the time,
And sincerely remember God,
And be present through the heart
And through the mind.
Dhikr is far better than trade.
Ah! If I told you what it is worth:
It is worth more than a kingdom and its ministers.
But people are distracted and neglect it.

– Aḥmad al-'Alawī [CAD/TW88]

Whoever madly desires to see the Beauty of the Friend, let him surrender himself to invocation.
Whoever wishes, like the moth, to dissolve in the candle, let him surrender himself to invocation.
The way which leads to the Beauty of the Friend is the invocation of those who invoke.
Whoever aims to reach the light of this Beauty, let him surrender himself to invocation.
Whoever is sincere in the way of God must give up his soul.
Whoever is fit to give up his soul let him surrender himself to invocation.
Whoever invokes with all his spirit and with all his heart will reach the One he invokes.
Whoever is reduced to nothing in invocation, let him surrender himself to invocation.
Whoever aspires to be invoking God, with every breath let him implore.
Whoever ardently desires to truly find the King, let him surrender himself to invocation.
This is the constant wish of suffering Üftāde!
That he who contemplates the Friend, renouncing all other, let him surrender himself to invocation.

– Meḥmed Muhyīddīn Üftāde [BAL/NG164]

Sufi Instruction

Knock on the door of the *dhikr*, seeking shelter with God and avowing your need of Him, with continual silence toward your fellows and the shepherding of your innermost being to guard it from converse with the lower self with every breath, if you desire to have spiritual sufficiency.

– Abū'l-Ḥasan ash-Shādhilī [DOU/TS181]

God is with the one who remembers Him and calls Him in his heart, and calls Him on his tongue, but we must realize that the *dhikr* of the heart is more perfect. The rememberer recites *dhikr* of the tongue in order to reflect the occurrence of the *dhikr* in his heart. When the love of God and His remembrance overwhelms the heart and the spirit, the tongue is moved and the seeker is brought near.

– Yahyā ibn Sharaf an-Nawawī [KAB/CI51]

O you who are dead at heart, you must practice constantly the remembrance of your Lord, the recitation of His Book, the study of the example of the Prophet, and attendance at sessions devoted to divine remembrance. Your hearts will then come back to life, just as the dead earth is brought back to life by the downpour of abundant rain upon it. When the heart is constantly engaged in the remembrance of God, it comes to be endowed with intimate experience, knowledge, the affirmation of Divine Unity, absolute trust, and a lack of interest in everything whatsoever apart from Him. The constant practice of remembrance produces good results that are constantly enduring in both this world and the hereafter.

– 'Abd al-Qādir al-Jīlānī [JIL/RC286]

Never be without the remembrance of God, for His remembrance provides the bird of the spirit with strength, feathers, and wings. If your goal becomes actualized completely, that is *Light upon Light* (24:35). But in any case, through the remembrance of God your inward [state] will be illuminated and you will achieve a degree of detachment from the world. For instance, look at the bird that wants to fly in heaven: Though it cannot reach heaven, moment by moment it soars farther from earth and higher than the other birds. Or consider a small box of musk whose opening is narrow: You put your hand into it, but you cannot bring out the musk; yet your hand becomes perfumed and your senses refreshed. So too is the remembrance of God: Even if you do not reach His Essence, yet His remembrance has numerous effects upon you. You actualize tremendous benefits by invoking Him.

– Jalāl ad-Dīn Rūmī [CHI/PL158]

The heart is like a mirror, and all these things surround it and have an effect upon it. Their traces constantly reach it. The praiseworthy effects that we have mentioned increase the polish, luminosity, and brilliance of the heart's mirror. Finally the plain evidence of the Truth sparkles within it and the desired goal of religion is unveiled. The Prophet alludes to this kind of heart with his words, "When God desires good for a servant, He appoints for him an admonisher from within his heart," and his words, "When a person has an admonisher within his heart, God has given him a protector." This is the heart within which the remembrance of God becomes firmly established. *In God's remembrance are hearts at peace* (13:28).

Blameworthy effects are like a dark smoke mounting up on the heart's mirror. The smoke keeps on piling up on it until the heart becomes dark and black, totally veiled from God. God calls this "sealing" and "rust." He says, *No indeed, but what they were earning has rusted upon the hearts* (83:14). Likewise He says, *Did We will, We would smite them because of their sins, sealing their hearts so that they do not listen* (7:100).

– Abū Ḥāmid al-Ghazālī [MUR/TI260]

The "Signs" as Reminder

Foundational Sources

In the creation of the heavens and the earth, and in the alternation of night and day, there are signs for men of understanding; those who remember God while standing, sitting, and lying down, and reflect upon the creation of the heavens and the earth.

– Qur'ān 3:191

How many a generation We destroyed before them that was stronger in valor than they, then they searched about in the land; was there any asylum? Surely in that there is a reminder to him who has a heart, or will give ear with a present mind.

– Qur'ān 50:37

Universal Remembrance

Foundational Sources

The seven heavens and the earth and all who dwell in them glorify Him; there is nothing that does not proclaim His praise, but you do

not understand their praises. Surely He is All-clement, All-forgiving.
– Qur'ān 17:44

All that is in the heavens and the earth glorifies God; He is the All-mighty, the All-wise.
– Qur'ān 57:1

Had God not driven back the people, some by the means of others, there had been destroyed cloisters and churches, synagogues and mosques, wherein God's Name is much mentioned.
– Qur'ān 22:40

Sufi Instruction

Whoever recollects God in reality, forgets all else beside Him, because all the creatures recollect Him, as is witnessed by those who experience a revelation. I experienced this state from evening prayer until one third of the night was over, and I heard the voices of the creatures in the praise of God, with elevated voices so that I feared for my mind. I heard the fishes who said, "Praised be the King, the Most Holy, the Lord."
– Dhul-Nūn al-Miṣrī [SCH/MD46]

The Qur'ān as Reminder

Foundational Sources

It is We who have sent down the Remembrance, and We watch over it.
– Qur'ān 15:9

And we have sent down to you [O Muḥammad] the Remembrance that you may make clear to mankind what was sent down to them; so that they may reflect.
– Qur'ān 16:44

God has sent down the fairest discourse as a Book . . . whereat the skins of those who fear their Lord tremble, and then their skins and hearts soften to the remembrance of God.
– Qur'ān 39:23

The People of Remembrance

Foundational Sources

And We sent none before you, but men to whom We made revelation—question the People of the Remembrance,[2] if you do not know.
– Qur'ān 21:7

And restrain yourself along with those who call upon their Lord at morning and evening, desiring His countenance; do not turn your eyes away from them, desiring the adornment of this life.
– Qur'ān 18:28

My true servant is the one who is in remembrance of Me when he faces his enemy.
– *Ḥadīth Qudsī* [HIR/DS60]

The best of you are those who, when they are seen, God is remembered.
– *Ḥadīth* [CHI/SD442]

The Prophet said, "The single-hearted are foremost." When asked, "O Messenger of God, who are the single-hearted?" he replied, "The men and women who remember God abundantly."
– *Ḥadīth* [KAB/GB100]

Sufi Aphorisms

The lights of some people precede their invocations, while the invocations of some people precede their lights. There is the invoker who invokes so that his heart be illumined; and there is the invoker whose heart has been illumined—and he invokes.
– Ibn 'Aṭā' Allāh al-Iskandarī [DAN/BW109]

Sufi Poetry

O God, the stars are shining;
All eyes have closed in sleep:

[2] Here, "People of the Remembrance" is a term closely related to "People of the Book," designating those communities, such as Jews and Christians, who have received earlier scriptures. However, the Book— both the Qur'ān and, by extension, earlier scriptures—is first and foremost a reminder to the community it addresses and thereby a motivating means by which individuals may turn to God in remembrance.

The kings have locked their doors.
Each lover is alone, in secret, with the one he loves.
And I am here too: alone, hidden from all of them—
With You.

– Rābi'a al-'Adawīya [UPT/DH52]

For lovers, the only lecturer is the beauty of the Beloved:
their only book and lecture and lesson is the Face.
Outwardly they are silent,
but their penetrating remembrance rises
to the high throne of their Friend.
Their only lesson is enthusiasm, whirling, and trembling,
not the precise points of law.

– Jalāl ad-Dīn Rūmī [HEL/JR40]

Sufi Instruction

God has said, *When you do not know, then inquire of the people of recollection* (16:43; 21:7). They are the people ever-mindful of God and the people of the divine transcendent unity and of understanding from God. They have not acquired this knowledge through the study of books, nor received it from one another by word of mouth. They were people of action and elegant deeds of devotion, so that when one of them was entirely dedicated to, and occupied with, God, he sought to labor in the service of the Master through deeds of the heart. They were with Him in seclusion before Him, remembering nothing but Him and occupying themselves with Him alone. And, when they appeared in public and someone questioned them, God inspired them with right guidance and accommodated them with the perfectly apposite response. He gave them wisdom as the heritage of the inward deeds arising from their pure hearts, pellucid minds, and lofty aspirations.

– Abū Tālib al-Makkī [REN/KG127]

The People of Heedlessness

Foundational Sources

The hypocrites seek to deceive God, but it is God who deceives them. When they stand up to pray they stand up lazily, showing off to the people and not remembering God save a little.

– Qur'ān 4:142

Nor obey him whose heart We have made neglectful of Our remembrance so that he follows his own lust, and his affair has become all excess.

– Qur'ān 18:28

The unbelievers whose eyes were covered against My remembrance, and they were not able to hear.

– Qur'ān 18:101

And he who blinds himself to the remembrance of the All-merciful, to him We appoint an evil one for a comrade.

– Qur'ān 43:36

So turn away from he who turns away from Our remembrance and seeks only the life of this world.

– Qur'ān 53:29

Satan has gained mastery of them, and caused them to forget the remembrance of God.

– Qur'ān 58:19

And be not as those who forgot God, so that He caused them to forget their own souls; those—they are the ungodly.

– Qur'ān 59:19

Sufi Poetry

When the teardrops have become friends of the rosary,
    then the rosary's work is blessed for you.
But if your heart is hardened, be sure
    that the thread of the rosary has turned into an infidel's girdle.

– Mīr Dard [SCH/TC92]

Sufi Instruction

Have you never read or heard His Words: *Only those are believers whose hearts thrill with awe at the remembrance of God* (8:2), and did you not know that the Prophet mentioned as being amongst his people "folk who enter Paradise and whose hearts are as the hearts of birds." Where are we to find those referred to in these utterances if not among the Rememberers? No doubt you tell yourself that you are one of them. So answer me this, with God as your witness: Are you one of *those who remember God much* (33:35), or of those *whom neither bartering nor selling diverteth from the remembrance of God* (24:37), or of those *whom neither their possessions nor children divert from the remembrance of God* (58:9), or of those *who remember God standing and sitting and reclining upon their sides* (3:191), or of those *whose hearts thrill with awe at the remembrance of God*, or of *those whose eyes overflow with tears when they hear what hath been revealed unto the Prophet* (5:83), or of those about whom the Prophet said: "The solitary ones take precedence, they who are utterly addicted to the remembrance of God," or of those who are called mad through acting on the Prophet's injunction: "Multiply remembrance of God until they say: 'Madman!'" or of those who are called pretenders because they act on his injunction: "Multiply remembrance of God until the hypocrites say: 'Verily ye are pretenders'"? Tell me, I beg you, which group you belong to. Are you one of the sayers or the said?

– Aḥmad al-'Alawī [LIN/SS94-95]

The Polish of the Heart

Foundational Sources

Those who believe and whose hearts find peace in the remembrance of God; truly it is in the remembrance of God that hearts find peace.

– Qur'ān 13:28

He who is so occupied with the remembrance of Me that he does not make petition to Me, I will give him the best of what I give to supplicants.

– *Ḥadīth Qudsī* [NAK/IS8]

Everything has a polish and the polish of hearts is the remembrance of God.

– *Ḥadīth* [KAB/CI48]

No Muslim takes up an abode in the mosques for the sake of prayer and invocation without God receiving him joyfully.

– *Ḥadīth* [CHI/PK438]

Remembrance of God is firm knowledge of one's belief, immunity from hypocrisy, a fortress against Satan, and a guarded refuge from the Fire.

– *Ḥadīth* [KAB/GB145]

People will not sit in the remembrance of God without the angels surrounding them, mercy covering them, tranquility descending on them, and God mentioning them among those who are with Him.

– *Ḥadīth* [FRI/SS132]

Sufi Aphorisms

The invocation is a tree whose fruit is gnosis.

– Ibn 'Aṭā' Allāh al-Iskandarī [DAN/KS76]

When the aspiring traveler clings to retreat and the remembrance of God's name, when he empties his heart of reflective thoughts, and when he sits in poverty at the door of his Lord with nothing, then God will bestow upon him and give him something of knowledge of Him, the divine mysteries, and the lordly sciences.

– Muḥyī ad-Dīn Ibn al-'Arabī [CHI/HP15]

Truth has been planted in the center of the heart as God's trust, entrusted to you for safekeeping. It becomes manifest with true repentance and with true efforts. Its beauty shines on the surface when one remembers God and does the *dhikr.* At the first stage one recites the name of God with one's tongue; then when the heart becomes alive one recites inwardly with the heart.

– 'Abd al-Qādir al-Jīlānī [BAY/SS10-11]

Sufi Poetry

If you mention His Name in the depths of a well,
He will make the well's depths the summit of paradise.

– Jalāl ad-Dīn Rūmī [CHI/PL159]

I have prayed so much that I myself turned into prayer—
Everyone who sees me begs a prayer from me.

– Jalāl ad-Dīn Rūmī [SCH/IW5]

O nightingale of the soul, I'm drunk from remembering you,
O footfall of heartache, I'm low from remembering you.
All the world's pleasures are trampled under foot
by the taste that comes to hand from remembering you.

– 'Abd ar-Raḥmān Jāmī [MUR/CG150]

If your every single breath became a prayer
You'd see atoms as angels and hear in each wind

The whirr of Love's wings, and feel in each moment
The Beloved pulling you into His heart.
– Jalāl ad-Dīn Rūmī [HAR/LG63]

His Name is the Spirit of spirits,
His invocation the ruby of the mines.
His love is in the soul,
He is both our refuge and our hope.
When I mention His Name,
good fortune arrives;
Then the Name becomes the Named—
without duality, without hesitation.
– Jalāl ad-Dīn Rūmī [CHI/PL159]

Those unable to grieve,
or to speak their love,
or to be grateful, those
who can't remember God
as the source of everything,

might be described as vacant wind,
or a cold anvil, or a group
of frightened old people.

Say the Name. Moisten your tongue
with praise, and be the spring ground,
waking. Let your mouth be given
its gold-yellow stamen like the wild rose's.

As you fill with wisdom,
and your heart with love,
there's no more thirst.

There's only an unselfed patience
waiting on the doorsill, a silence
which doesn't listen to advice
from people passing in the street.
– Hakim Sanā'ī [KHA/HP18]

Oh my God, grant the heart illumination through Your invocation
Displaying Your sweet Beauty in the affirmation of Unity, oh God!

Guide Your invocation as the means to Your Essence.
Those who attained always attained through invocation.

Give our souls eternal life through Your invocation
That by invocation the one who is saved from annihilation finds
 true existence.

May His beauty be displayed to the eyes, may the lights of the
 Essence be revealed!
In light drown Your lovers, oh God!

That which silence grants them is the promise of His Beauty.
For Him they always sing grace and praise.

They are hoping today to see Your sweet Beauty.
From beginning to end they have no other desire.

Free yourself from all otherness, oh suffering Üftāde!
That in rejoining the light of His Beauty you find serenity.
– Meḥmed Muhyīddīn Üftāde [BAL/NG161]

The light of the senses and spirit of our ancestors
 doesn't perish like the grass,
but, like the stars and moonbeams,
 they vanish in the radiance of the Sun.
It's like the naked man who jumped into the water,
 so that he might escape from the hornets' stings:
the hornets circled above him, and whenever he put out his head
 they would not spare him.
The water is recollection of God,
 and the hornet is the thought, during this time,
  of such-and-such a woman or man.
Hold your breath in the water of remembrance,
 so you may be freed from old thoughts and temptations.
After that, you will assume the nature of that pure water,
 entirely from head to foot.
As the noxious hornet flees from the water,
 so will it be afraid of approaching you.
After that be far from the water, if you wish;
 for in your inmost soul you are of the same nature as the water.
Those persons then who have passed from the world
 are not non-existent but are absorbed in the attributes of God,
  even as the star disappears in the presence of the sun.
– Jalāl ad-Dīn Rūmī [HEL/JR58]

Sufi Instruction

The first person I met on the Way was Abū Ja'far Aḥmad al-'Uryanī. He had arrived in Seville at a time when I had only just started to become acquainted with this noble Path. I was the first of those who hastened to him. I found a man totally devoted to invocation (*dhikr*). I presented myself to him and he knew immediately the spiritual need which had brought me to him. He asked me: "Are you firmly resolved to follow the Way of God?" I replied: "The servant is resolved but it is God who determines the matter." He then said to me: "Close your door, break all ties, and keep company with the All-Bounteous; He will speak to you without a veil." I put this into practice until I received illumination.

– Muḥyī ad-Dīn Ibn al-'Arabī [ADD/QR49-50]

There are different levels of remembrance, and each has different ways. Some are expressed outwardly with audible voice, some felt inwardly, silently, from the center of the heart. At the beginning one should declare in words what one remembers. Then stage by stage the remembrance spreads throughout one's being—descending to the heart, then rising to the soul; then still further it reaches the realm of the secrets; further to the hidden; to the most hidden of the hidden. How far the remembrance penetrates, the level it reaches, depends solely on the extent to which God in His bounty has guided one.

– 'Abd al-Qādir al-Jīlānī [BAY/SS45]

If you ask me, oh my brother, which are the signs of the Path, I would answer you very clearly and without ambiguity. The Path is to look at truth and break with falsity, it is to turn your face to the living universe, to despise the earthly dignities, to free your mind from any ambition of glory and fame, to stoop to His service, to purify your soul from evil and strengthen it with reason, to leave the house of those who talk too much and go to the one where people are silent and to travel from God's manifestations to God's Attributes and from there to His Knowledge. Then, at that moment, you will have crossed the world of mysteries and arrived at the door of Poverty. When you are Poverty's friend, your deep soul will have become a penitent heart. Then, God will extract Poverty from your heart, and when Poverty is gone from there, God will stay in your heart.

– Hakim Sanā'ī [VIT/RS77]

The Passing from All but the Remembered

Sufi Aphorisms

To turn towards God is to turn away from the creature and to turn towards the creature is to turn away from God.

– Ibn 'Aṭā' Allāh al-Iskandarī [BUR/LS3]

The real significance of the remembrance lies in one's being detached from remembrance and joined to the One remembered in the *dhikr*, and detached from everything except Him.

– Abū'l-Ḥasan ash-Shādhilī [DOU/TS173]

Sufi Poetry

So constantly are you in my stricken soul and sleepless eyes
That whatsoever should appear from afar, I should think that it was you.

– 'Abd ar-Raḥmān Jāmī [SCH/TV60]

Sufi Instruction

Do not abandon the invocation because you do not feel the Presence of God therein. For your forgetfulness *of* the invocation of Him is worse than your forgetfulness *in* the invocation of Him. Perhaps He will take you from an invocation with forgetfulness to one with vigilance, and from one with vigilance to one with the Presence of God, and from one with the Presence of God to one wherein everything but the Invoked is absent. *And that is not difficult for God* (14:20).

– Ibn 'Aṭā' Allāh al-Iskandarī [DAN/BW58-59]

The people who are aware that the mighty and glorious Lord is watching them are ashamed before the gaze of the Real, fearing lest they should revere anything beside that which He has commanded. Anyone who truly remembers the mighty and glorious Lord forgets the remembrance of anything else in recalling Him. And if anyone forgets the remembrance of things in the remembrance of the Real, everything watches over him, because for him the Lord most high takes the place of everything.

– Yūsuf ibn al-Ḥusayn [LOS/AM307]

The first stage for that one who has found the knowledge of unification and the assurance of that, is that there passes from his heart the remembrance of all things and he becomes alone with God Most

High. For the first stage of unification is that the servant gives up everything and returns all things to Him to Whom they belong and that He is in control of them and makes them subject to Himself. So then the remembrance of all things passes from the servant's heart and the remembrance of God Most High takes possession of it—the heart—and the remembrance of things passes from his heart in the remembrance of God Most Glorious.

– Abū Sa'īd Aḥmad al-Kharrāz [SMI/RM19]

There are three types of invokers. One invokes God with his tongue while his heart is heedless: such is the invocation (*dhikr*) of the "wrongdoer," who knows nothing of the invocation or the One Invoked. Another invokes Him with his tongue while his heart is attentive: such is the *dhikr* of the "frugal" and the state of the "hireling," who seeks a reward but whose seeking is excusable. The third type invokes God with his heart; his heart is filled with God, and his tongue utters no invocation: "He who knows God, his tongue flags." Such is the *dhikr* of the "foremost."[3] His tongue has entered the mystery of the *dhikr*, the *dhikr* is in the mystery of the One Invoked; his heart is in the mystery of Love; Love is in the mystery of Light; his Spirit is in the mystery of direct vision [of the Unseen]; and direct vision is far from being describable!

– Rashīd ad-Dīn Maybudī [LEW/CP531-532]

The Passing from the Remembrance

Sufi Aphorisms

Sufism is a remembrance, then a rapture, then neither this nor that, until it seems that it does not exist.

– Abū'l-Qāsim al-Junayd [LOS/AM354]

Dhikr is, in its reality, the progressive power of the Named on the heart, while the *dhikr* itself wears away and disappears.

– Abū Ḥāmid al-Ghazālī [VIT/RS99]

For thirty years I was hidden from God. My absence from Him was my recollection (*dhikr*) of Him. When I refrained (from *dhikr*), I saw Him in every state, to such a degree that it was as if I were He.

– Bāyazīd al-Bisṭāmī [ERN/WE26]

[3] The "foremost" are designated in the Qur'ān (56:10) as those possessed of particular spiritual excellence or perfection who are "brought near" to God.

Sufi Instruction

You must know that God removed all the veils of ignorance and brought people to the state of vision through their continuous *dhikr*. The first stage is *dhikr* of the tongue, then the *dhikr* of the heart, then the appearance of the Divine Presence in the reciter of *dhikr*, making him no longer need to do *dhikr*.

– Abū Ḥāmid al-Ghazālī [KAB/CI55]

There is no remembrance along with witnessing. Hence the rememberers must be veiled. Although [a *ḥadīth* says] "God sits with those who remember Him," this is from behind the veil of remembrance. Whenever someone's object of seeking is behind a veil, he cannot be at ease. When the veil is lifted, witnessing occurs, and the remembrance disappears in the self-disclosure of the Remembered.

– Muḥyī ad-Dīn Ibn al-'Arabī [CHI/SS59]

As the aspirant sits in solitude, saying continuously with his tongue "Allāh, Allāh," keeping his thought on it, he eventually comes to a state in which his effort to move his tongue drops off and it looks as if the word were flowing on his tongue all by itself. Then, let him adhere to this until any trace of motion is removed from his tongue and he finds his mind persevering in *dhikr*. Then, let him still adhere to this until the image of the word, its letters and shape are effaced from his mind and there remains the idea of the word alone in the mind, clinging to it, as if it were glued to the mind, without separating from it.

– Abū Ḥāmid al-Ghazālī [NAK/ISxxvi]

The Passing Away of the Rememberer

Foundational Sources

Do not remember God absent-mindedly, nor forget Him in distraction; rather, remember Him with perfect remembrance, a remembrance in which your heart and tongue are in harmony, and what you conceal conforms with what you reveal. But you will not remember Him according to the true reality of the remembrance until you forget your own soul in your remembrance.

– 'Alī ibn Abī Ṭālib [KAZ/JR162]

Truly, God has a drink for His friends. When they drink it, they are intoxicated; and when they are intoxicated, they are enraptured; and when they are enraptured, they are blessed; and when they are blessed they dissolve; and when they dissolve, they are free; and when they are free, they devote themselves purely; and when they devote themselves purely, they seek; and when they seek, they find; and when they find, they arrive; and when they arrive, they are at one; there is no difference between them and their Beloved.

– ʿAlī ibn Abī Ṭālib [KAZ/JR167-168]

Sufi Aphorisms

Whoever remembers his Lord constantly always forgets his self.

– Mulay al-ʿArabī ad-Darqāwī [ABD/DW288]

True remembrance is the annihilation of the rememberer in the Remembered.

– Abū'l-Ḥusayn an-Nūrī [CHI/SS59]

The reality of remembrance is the extinction of the rememberer in remembrance and of remembrance in the contemplation of the remembered.

– Abū'l-Qāsim al-Junayd [LOS/AM360]

True perfection is that the heart be emptied of all remembrance (*dhikr*) and consciousness such that only the Object of Remembrance remains.

– ʿAzīz ad-Dīn Nasafī [LEW/WS143]

Sufi Poetry

Remember God so much that you are forgotten.
Let the caller and the called disappear;
Be lost in the Call.

– Jalāl ad-Dīn Rūmī [HEL/LS65]

I would, so overflowing is my love for Him,
Remember Him perpetually, yet my remembrance—
Wondrous to tell—is vanished into ecstasy,
And wonder upon wonder, even ecstasy,
With memory's self, in nearness-farness vanished is.

– Abū'l-Ḥusayn an-Nūrī [LIN/SP18]

From my words take fruits which yield pleasure and delight,
Whose fragrance wafts forth with the redolence of musk.

Having been guided to the remembrance of God, pursue it steadfastly,
For in it both hearts and mouths find sweetness and relief.

Let your adornment be devotion to Him, for the wise soul,
My friend, is the one whose devotion to Him is his adornment.

Let your thoughts labor in His kingdom,
Absorbed in unearthing its meaning.

Remove your sandals as one realized [in the divine realities],
As one who forswears both universes in his upward spiritual trek.

Be annihilated even to your annihilation,
For herein lies true subsistence, and then will you behold Him.

And when He appears to you, know that you are not He,
Nor, indeed, are you anything but He.

Two entities which have not been united, but herein lies
A mystery which we are hard pressed to explain.

You who hear what we have said:
Should one's heart not ponder what one's ears have perceived?

Remove the veil, the veil of your senses,
And the mystery whose grandeur you've failed to perceive will appear.

The Divine is the most sublime entity that could ever be known,
Hence, the blindness of those who fail to see Him.

It is through Him that those endowed with discernment see Him,
And indeed, He hasn't been out of their sight for a moment.

After all, how could He be absent when nothing but He exists?
Yet the very intensity of His presence conceals Him from view!
– Abū'l-Ḥasan ash-Shādhilī [ROB/SB313-315]

Sufi Instruction

By giving himself up to prayer and to the remembrance of God [the aspirant] is carried from his own forgetfulness to God's presence, and from His presence to the unveiling of that which is hidden, until he becomes extinguished in the One invoked.

– Fāṭimah al-Yashruṭiyya [CAD/TW118]

Have you ever had a time in recollection when you were not a thing remembered? If this is not the case, then you will never perfect true recollection, because one of the characteristics of *dhikr* is the forgetting of everything besides God, as He says in His book: *And remember your Lord when you have forgotten* (18:24), that is, forgotten everything but the Lord.

– 'Alā' ad-Dawla as-Simnānī [ELI/TC133]

Trust in God until the remembrance of Him (*dhikr*) has completely overpowered you; for creatures are of no use to you. . . . Every spiritual truth that fails to extinguish the traces of the creature, is no (real) truth. . . . Spiritual poverty is a pointer to the Divine Unity and a proof of detachment from multiplicity. The meaning of poverty is simply this: that you take cognizance of nothing but Him.

– Abū Madyan [BUR/FC133]

The *dhikr* has four aspects: a *dhikr* meaning the act of remembering; a *dhikr* meaning the object of your remembrance; a *dhikr* that evokes your remembrance; and a *dhikr* that causes you to be remembered. . . . The fourth, a *dhikr* that causes you to be remembered, is God's remembrance of His servants, in which nothing depends on the servant, although his tongue pronounces it. In this situation he is effaced in the act of remembrance or in the One remembered, the Lofty and Most High, for whenever you are admitted into this state, the rememberer becomes the remembered, and the remembered the rememberer. This is what one has to end with while following the [Sufi] way, and God is better and more abiding.

– Abū'l-Ḥasan ash-Shādhilī [DOU/TS163]

As Gabriel told the Apostle [Muḥammad] that God said: "My servant continually seeks access to Me by means of works of supererogation until I love him; and when I love him, I am his ear and his eye and his hand and his heart and his tongue: through Me he hears and sees and speaks and grasps," i.e., in remembering Me he is enraptured by the remembrance of Me, and his own "acquisition" is annihilated so as to have no part in his remembrance, and My remembrance overpowers his remembrance, and the relationship of humanity is entirely removed from his remembrance: then My remembrance is his remembrance, and in his rapture he becomes even as Bāyazīd in the hour when he said: "Glory to me! how great is my majesty!" These words were the outward sign of his speech, but the speaker was God.

– Abū'l-Hasan 'Alī al-Hujwīrī [NIC/RM254]

Remembrance pronounced in words is but a declaration that the heart has not forgotten God. The inward silent remembrance is a movement of the emotions. The remembrance of the heart is through feeling in oneself the manifestation of God's might and beauty, while the remembrance of the soul is through the enlightenment of the divine light generated by God's might and beauty. The remembrance of the level of the secret realm is through the ecstasy received from beholding the divine secrets. The remembrance of the hidden realm brings one to *the place of truth in the presence of a Sovereign Omnipotent* (54:55). The remembrance at the final level that is called "the most hidden of the hidden" brings one to a state of annihilation of the self and unification with the truth. In reality none other than God knows the state of the one who has penetrated into that realm containing all knowledge, which is the end of all and everything. *Surely He knows the secret and what is yet more hidden* (20:7).

– 'Abd al-Qādir al-Jīlānī [BAY/SS45-46]

V. Realization of Unity: The Manifold Aspects of *Fanā'-Baqā'*

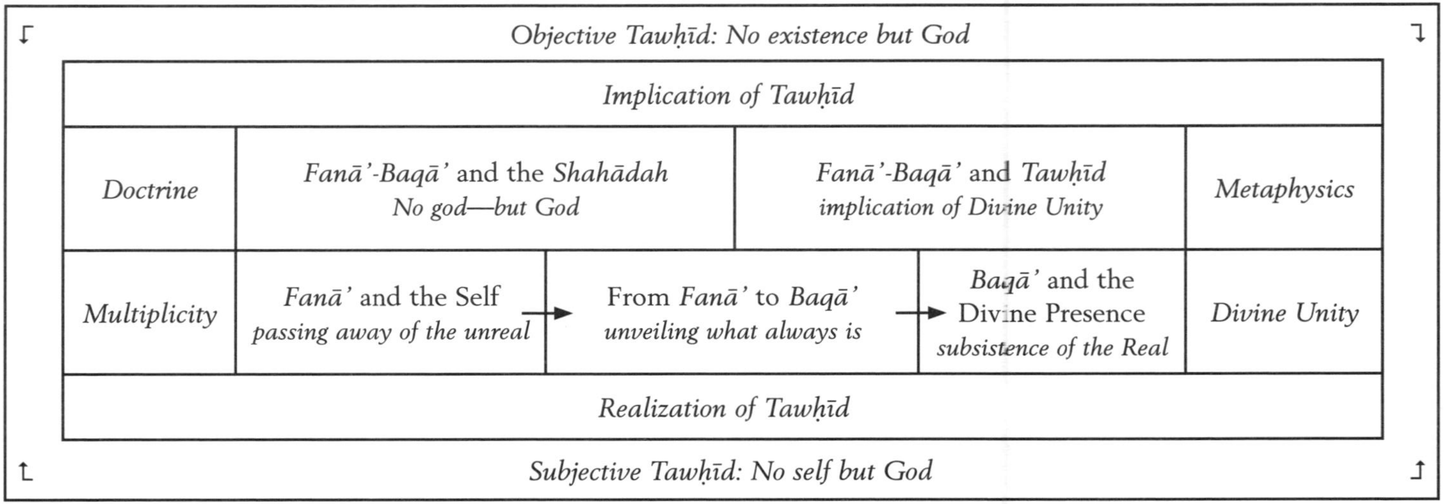

V. Realization of Unity: The Stations of *Fanā'* and *Baqā'*

Overview: *Fanā'* and *Baqā'*

The words of the *Shahādah* give testimony to the essential nature of reality, but as words alone this testimony is necessarily mediated and indirect. The *Shahādah* is, for the faithful, a promise yet to be fulfilled, for while multitudes have borne witness that "There is no god but God," few have truly and directly witnessed this in their very being. And yet those few have and, further, have left their traces, particularly in the conjoined spiritual realizations of *fanā'* and *baqā'*, exalted examples of what the Sufi tradition terms "stations" (*maqāmāt*), representing the assimilation to one's being of various virtues or internal states.

Although the Sufi tradition also speaks of "union" with God, such a means of expression is inherently problematic in the context of the metaphysics of the tradition, for such a "union" must necessarily involve a precedent dualism that the doctrine of *tawḥīd* ultimately denies. Although an apparent multiplicity persists at the level of the created order, this multiplicity cannot persist in the Divine Itself. Put more pointedly, how can anything achieve "union" with That which is alone real? Human existence is in fact founded upon a metaphysical paradox, one which *fanā'* and *baqā'* throw into sharp relief, for we are at once entirely other, apart, and dissimilar to God—what the tradition speaks of as *tanzīh*, or God's transcendence—while also being alike, intimate, and similar to God—what the tradition speaks of as *tashbīh*, or God's immanence.

The Sufi metaphysician Ibn al-'Arabī succinctly describes the paradoxical situation of the created order as "He / not He," in relation to which God stands as both immanent and transcendent. Taken in this understanding, in relation to the Divine transcendence, we are not nor have ever been, whereas in relation to the Divine immanence, we are, but through Him. We, as part of the created order, are similarly bound up as at once "He / not He." This is the actual state of affairs, although in the context of the apparent self-subsistence, independence, and multiplicity of the created order we do not normally realize this. The conjoined stations of *fanā'* and *baqā'* may be understood as simply a realization of our actual situation. Not an alteration, for nothing has altered—and this too is a reason not to speak of "union"—nor even an experience—which requires an independent "experiencer"—but a recognition or realization of what is.

This of course poses a certain danger of misunderstanding if not misappropriation, particularly with regard to *baqā'*, for an "ecstatic locution," such as al-Ḥallāj's famous "I am God," can be readily taken as a claim of self-divinization, the exact opposite of its actual significance. In a very real sense, *fanā'* and *baqā'* form the truest and most sincere witnessing of the reality of God and thereby of the *Shahādah*, for ultimately there is only one witness, that of God Himself. If the stations of *fanā'* and *baqā'* bear respective witness to the "no god" and "but God" of the *Shahādah*, then in their conjoined recognition of the Real, they demonstrate the truth of *tawḥīd*, that this Reality is one.

The very terminology of *fanā'*, the passing away or annihilation of the self, would seem to indicate a change of condition, but a clearer understanding is that it is the passing away of an apparent and illusory subsistence, of that which stands in relation to God as a borrowed reality, ultimately as an unreality. What is thereby revealed is the Real, which truly subsists and always has done so, as the terminology of *baqā'* implies. In this sense also, although *fanā'* and *baqā'* have the appearance of two distinct realizations, they are necessarily conjoined, being in fact two aspects of the same realization: to unveil the self in its absence is necessarily to reveal the Divine in Its presence.

Fanā'-Baqā' and the *Shahādah*

Foundational Sources

And call not upon another god with God; there is no god but He. Everything is perishing except His Face.

– Qur'ān 28:88

The truest verse sung by the Arabs is the line of Labīd, "Is not everything other than God unreal?"

– *Ḥadīth* [CHI/PK439]

Sufi Aphorisms

Only God has the right to say "I," for whoever says "I" will not reach the level of gnosis.

– Abū Sa'īd Aḥmad al-Kharrāz [SCH/MD55]

In that glory is no "I" or "We" or "Thou." "I," "We," "Thou," and "He" are all one thing.

– Ḥusayn Ibn Manṣūr al-Ḥallāj [NIC/MI152]

True *fanā'* is the vision of the relation of the worshipper to God Most Glorious, and true *baqā'* is the vision of the relation of God to all worship.

– Ya'qūb an-Nahrajūrī [SMI/SE215]

You are not veiled from God by the existence of something that exists with Him since there is nothing which exists with Him. You are veiled from Him by the illusion that something exists with Him.

– Ibn 'Aṭā' Allāh al-Iskandarī [ABD/DW52]

Adorn me with Your unity, clothe me with Your subjectivity, and take me up to Your oneness, until when Your creation sees me they say "We have seen You" and You will be *that*, and I will not be there.

– Bāyazīd al-Bisṭāmī [SEL/EI216]

Everything other than He is in the midst of three things: yesterday's nonexistence, today's lostness, and tomorrow's naughtedness. Thus, all are nonexistent except for Him, yet existent through Him. Thus all are His Existence.

– Khwāja 'Abd Allāh Anṣārī [NUR/SF113]

Sufi Poetry

O you who seek God every day,
Do you not know it, where God is?
He is present wherever *I* am,
Wherever *I* look, He is there.

– Yūnus Emre [SCH/TV169]

We were letters, exalted! not yet uttered,
Held aloft in the keep of the Highest of Summits,
I Therein am Thou, and we are Thou,
And Thou art He, and All is in He is He—
Ask of any that so far hath reached.

– Muḥyī ad-Dīn Ibn al-'Arabī [LIN/SP64]

Everything is perishing but His Face (55:26)—
since you are not in His Face, do not seek to be.

When someone is annihilated in Our Face,
Everything is perishing no longer applies to him.
For he is in *but God*, he has passed beyond *no god.*
Whoever is in *but* has not been annihilated.
– Jalāl ad-Dīn Rūmī [CHI/SS88]

One with Thee make me, O my One, through Oneness
Faithed in sincerity no path can reach.
I am the Truth, and Truth, for Truth, is Truth,
Robed in Its Essence, thus beyond separation.
Lo, they are manifest, the brightnesses
That from Thy dawning Presence scintillate,
Each gleam a brilliance like the lightning flash.
– Ḥusayn Ibn Manṣūr al-Ḥallāj [LIN/SP28]

If He is in sight wherever you look,
why cast a blind eye
when it comes to yourself?

The Real said to you
I'm wherever you turn (2:115)—

So why don't you take
a closer look at yourself?
– Dārā Shikūh [FID/LA134]

If you dwell with the Friend
in genuine intimacy
then, in the whole world,
you will see
the incomparable God.

Since the whole world
is the living mirror of God,
it is impossible to see anything
aside from God.
– Sa'd ad-Dīn Ḥamawī [FID/LA127]

On Unity's Way:
no infidelity
no faith.
Take one step
away from yourself and—
behold!—the Path!

You, soul of the world,
    must choose the road
        of Divine Submission
then sit with anyone you like
    —even a black snake—
        but not your self!

– Abū Sa'īd Ibn Abī'l-Khayr [WIL/DU32]

Sufi Instruction

Save Thee, I see naught in the two worlds, for in truth Thou alone exist in this world and in that. From everlasting Thou was and changeless shall be: unto eternity is Thy Being and shall be forever. O Thou Who did make manifest both time and place, Thou have created both the soul of man and the universe wherein he dwells, and Thou does cause the spheres to revolve and does make the hearts of thousands to be filled with awe and amazement at Thy manifestation of Thyself.

Now I am made one with Thee and from that Union my heart is consumed with rapture and my tongue is all bewildered. By union, I have been merged in Unity, I am become altogether apart from all else. I am Thou and Thou art I—nay, not I, all is altogether Thou. I have passed away, "I" and "Thou" no more exist. We have become one and I have become altogether Thou.

By union with Thee, I have become the perfected gnostic and now the gnostic has vanished away and I have become altogether the Creative Truth. I am free from both pride and passion and desire. I reveal the Divine Mysteries and thereby I fill the lovers of God throughout the world with amazement and a hundred thousand creatures remain astonished at me. All forms are consumed in the flames, when the candle of Union with Him is set alight and blazes up.

When the paintings are hidden, you will see the Painter. O brother, I will tell you the mystery of mysteries. Know, then, that painting and Painter are one! When your faith is made perfect, you will never see yourself, save in Him.

– Farīd ad-Dīn 'Aṭṭār [SMI/RM61-62]

For thirty years God Most High was my mirror, now I am my own mirror and that which I was I am no more, for "I" and "God" represents polytheism, a denial of His Unity. Since I am no more, God Most High is His own mirror. Behold, now I say that God is the mirror of myself, for with my tongue He speaks and I have passed away.

– Bāyazīd al-Bisṭāmī [SMI/RM15]

On the path of God there is no room for "This is mine" and "That belongs to me." This path is the way of obliteration and extinction. At the outset, when faith is still weak, the believer makes his affirmation in the words: "There is none worthy of worship but God." But in the final stage, when faith is strong, he utters the words: "There is none worthy of worship but You" because he is addressing One who is actually Present.

– 'Abd al-Qādir al-Jīlānī [JIL/RC158-159]

It is at this point that the reality of *lā ilāha illā 'Llāh* ["There is no god but God"] manifests itself, for the idol of existence totally vanishes and the monarchy of divinity establishes itself throughout the realm.

> How might we become separate from ourselves,
> Thou and I depart, and God alone remains?

When this reality appeared in the realm of the Muḥammadan being—peace be upon him!—God addressed to him this phrase: *So know that there is no god but God* (47:19). Until this station is witnessed, knowledge of the reality of *lā ilāha illā 'Llāh* will not appear. The verse continues, *and ask forgiveness for thy sin* (47:19). That is to say, "for the sin of thy existence." "Thy existence is a sin to which no other may be compared" (Rābi'a).

– Najm ad-Dīn Rāzī [ALG/GB320]

When Ḥallāj's love for God reached its utmost limit, he became his own enemy and he naughted himself. He said, "I am the Real," that is, "I have been annihilated; the Real remains, nothing else." This is extreme humility and the utmost limit of servanthood. It means, "He alone *is*." To make a false claim and to be proud is to say, "You are God and I am the servant." In this way you are affirming your own existence, and duality is the necessary result. If you say, "He is the Real," that too is duality, for there cannot be a "He" without an "I." Hence the Real said, "I am the Real." Other than He, nothing else existed. Ḥallāj had been annihilated, so those were the words of the Real.

– Jalāl ad-Dīn Rūmī [CHI/SS17]

When the mystic enters into the pure and absolute Unicity of the One and into the Kingdom of the One and Alone, mortals reach the end of their ascent. For there is no ascent beyond it, since ascent involves multiplicity, implying, as it does, an ascent from somewhere and an ascent to somewhere, and when multiplicity has been eliminated,

Unity is established and relationship ceases, signs are effaced, there remains neither height nor depth, nor one to descend or ascend. No higher ascent for the soul is possible, for there is no height beyond the highest and no multiplicity in face of the Unity, and since multiplicity has been effaced, no further ascent.

– Abū Ḥāmid al-Ghazālī [SMI/RM47]

Union with God is far from created things. To be His friend is to become a stranger to oneself. When it becomes possible for the contingent to pass away, nothing but the essential remains. Unity is like a sea—look and see how a drop from that ocean has found so many forms and has been given so many names, mist and water and rain and dew and clay, plant, animal, and finally, man in his perfection. All come from one drop, at the last as at the first: from that drop all these things were fashioned. The phantoms pass away: in one moment there remains—in all places—only the Creative Truth. At that moment of time you come near to Him: parted from self, you can join the Beloved. In God there is no duality. In that Presence "I" and "we" and "you" do not exist. "I" and "you" and "we" and "He" become one. Since in the Unity there is no distinction, the Quest and the Way and the Seeker become one.

– Sa'd ud-Dīn Maḥmūd Shabistarī [SMI/RM76]

God said: "What you said is true (*ḥaqq*), what you heard is true, what you saw is true, what you verified is true." I said, "Yes! You are the Truth, and the Truth sees by the Truth; You are the Truth, and the Truth verifies by the Truth. The Truth hears the Truth by the Truth. You are the Hearer and You are the One who makes hear, You are the Truth and You are the one who makes true, there is no god but You." He said, "What are you, if not the Truth? You speak by the Truth." So I said, "No! You are the Truth, and Your speech is true, and the Truth is true by You. You are You, there is no god but You." Then He said to me, "Who are you?" I said to Him, "Who are You?" He said, "I am the Truth" (*anā al-ḥaqq*). Then I said, "I am through You." He said, "If you exist through Me, then I am you and you are I." Then I said, "Don't beguile me by Yourself from Yourself. Yes! You are You, there is no god but You." Then my attributes became the Attributes of divine Lordship, and my tongue the Tongue of attestation of unity (*tawḥīd*), and my attributes were He; truly, "he is He," there is no god but He.

– Bāyazīd al-Bisṭāmī [ERN/WE44]

Know that gnosis means "knowledge of the state." It is this that takes the one who possesses it out of himself, and is found in all parts of the heart, including its deepest corners. In all states the possessor of gnosis perceives his Lord in [the complementary Divine aspects of] Beauty and Glory:

> I have seen Beauty, I have seen Glory,
> My Lover and Beloved, in any case.
>
> Yet the gnostics have been annihilated;
> They perceive nothing but the Imperious, the Most Exalted.
>
> They see what is other than Him destroyed in actuality,
> In the present, in the past, and in the future.

The sun of the day sets by night, but the sun of the heart is never absent. One who perceives the interiors of vessels comprehends the secrets of the Divine Mysteries. But one who sees the Sun of the Beloved is absent from near or far, and finds nothing but the All-Hearing and the All-Answering.

It is impossible for one who sees Him to perceive anything apart from Him, for that which is other than Him does not see Him. The gnostic feels no sadness at realization. I have seen the Beloved with the eye of His heart, by means of the hidden secret: There is no god but God.

– Abū Ya'zā ibn Maymūn ad-Dukkālī [COR/AM180]

Fanā'-Baqā' and *Tawḥīd*

Foundational Sources

And say: "The Real has come and the unreal has vanished away; surely the unreal is ever certain to vanish."

– Qur'ān 17:81

If you are not, you will see Him, for He sees you.[1]

– *Ḥadīth* [CHI/SD438]

[1] From the third part of the famous *ḥadīth* of Jibrīl (Gabriel), in which Muḥammad was questioned by Gabriel concerning the quality of *iḥsān* (spiritual beauty or excellence) to which he replied, "Doing what is beautiful is to worship God as if you see Him, for if you do not see Him, [know that] He sees you." Ibn al-'Arabī employs a grammatically equivalent rendering of the Arabic *ḥadīth*, "If you are not, you will see Him, for He sees you," indicating thereby how the very sense of selfhood may commonly obscure awareness of the Divine Presence. Ibn al-'Arabī follows with a poetic passage that begins: "So, if you are not, you will see Him, but if you are, you will not see Him" [CHI/SD212].

Sufi Poetry

The whole show but one
  lone puppeteer
hid behind his
  screen of art.
He tears it away
  reveals himself alone
and all illusions
  vanish into nothing.

– Ibn al-Fārid [CHI/DF103]

My sight has disappeared into His sight,
and it is annihilated to every vanishing thing.
I realized that other-than-Him does not exist,
And departed in delight immediately.

– 'Abd ar-Raḥmān al-Majdhūb [ABD/DW156]

When You made a show of unity, I was lost to myself.
Neither intimacy nor union, stage nor goal, body nor soul remain.
Nor is there love of any kind, nor place, nor being.
In that instant, Bāhū, I was faced with the secret of divine unity.

– Sulṭān Bāhū [ELI/DB36]

To exalt oneself is to claim partnership with God.
Unless you have died and become living through Him,
you are an enemy seeking to hold the power.
But when you have come to live through God,
that which you have become is in truth He:
it is no longer copartnership, but absolute Unity.

– Jalāl ad-Dīn Rūmī [HEL/JR78]

Those taken at Alast[2]
  are still drunk from that day's covenant.
They are foot-bound in the station of pain,
  open-handed in throwing away their lives.

[2] "Alast," or the "Day of Alast," refers to the Qur'ānic passage describing the pre-eternal covenant between God and a humanity yet to be created: "And when thy Lord took from the Children of Adam, from their loins, their seed, and made them testify touching themselves, 'Am I not your Lord?' (*alastu bi-Rabbikum*) They said, 'Yes, we testify'— lest you should say on the Day of Resurrection, 'As for us, we were heedless of this'" (7:171).

Quick they go and with one stride
    they jump the river of time.
Annihilated from themselves and subsistent in the Friend,
    this is strange: they are and are not.
These are the people who have reached *tawḥīd*—
    the rest all worship themselves.

– Naṣīr ad-Dīn Qūnawī [CHI/FP65]

He who contemplates God through creatures
Loses sight of them by disappearing in Him
And there remains naught but the Divine.
The knowledge of Unity is like fire—
It enflames everything it comes upon,
And by this very act purifies it.
Do not forsake your soul, nor be its enemy—
Be its companion instead and try to search
What it holds within.
There is not a single atom in the universe that
Carries not in it one of the Names of the One Adored.

– Aḥmad al-'Alawī [CAD/TW104]

A man knocked at the door of his beloved.
"Who are you, trusted one?" thus asked the friend.
He answered: "I!" The friend said: "Go away,
Here is no place for people raw and crude!"
What, then, could cook the raw and rescue him
But separation's fire and exile's flame?
The poor man went to travel a whole year
And burned in separation from his friend,
And he matured, was cooked and burnt, returned
And carefully approached the friend's abode.
He walked around it now in cautious fear
Lest from his lips unfitting words appear.
His friend called out: "Who is there at my door?"
The answer: "You, dear, *you* are at the door!"
He said: "Come in, now that you are all I—
There is no room in this house for two 'I's!"

– Jalāl ad-Dīn Rūmī [SCH/IW112]

I have found the soul of souls.
Let this soul of mine be taken.

I've forgotten gain and loss.
Let this shop of mine be plundered.

I've passed beyond my very self.
I've removed the veils before me.

I am together with the Friend.
Let these doubts of mine fall away.

My own ego abandoned me.
The Friend took everything I had.

Those who give and take are friends.
Let this language of mine be jumbled.

I cut all ties and went to the Friend.
I fell in with God. Let my poems be scattered.

I became tired of twoness
and ate at the table of Oneness.

I drank the wine of suffering.
Let all my remedies be thrown out.

Since this journey of Being began,
the Friend has rushed to meet us.

Light has filled the ruins of this heart.
Let this universe of mine be shattered.

I have passed up dreams.
I have tired of summers and winters.

I have found the Gardener of flowers.
Let this garden of mine be dug up.

Yūnus, you say it well,
smooth as honey.

I have found the honey of honeys.
Let this hive of mine be given away.
– Yūnus Emre [HEL/DS65]

What shall I do, O Muslims?
I do not recognize myself. . . .

I am neither Christian nor Jew,
nor Magian, nor Muslim.
I am not of the East, nor the West,
not of the land, nor the sea.
I am not from nature's mine,
nor from the circling stars.
I am neither of earth nor water,
neither of wind nor fire.
I am not of the empyrean,
nor of the dust on this carpet.
I am not of the deep, nor from behind.
I am not of India or China,
not of Bulgaria, nor Saqsin;
I am not of the kingdom of Iraqain,
nor of the land of Khorasan.
I am not of this world nor the next,
not of heaven, nor of purgatory.
My place is the placeless,
my trace is the traceless.
It is not the body nor is it the soul,
for I belong to the soul of my love.
I have put duality away
and seen the two worlds as one.
One I seek, One I know.
One I see, One I call.
He is the First, He is the Last.
He is the Outward, He is the Inward.

– Jalāl ad-Dīn Rūmī [HEL/LS56-57]

Sufi Instruction

I came out of Bāyazīd-ness as a snake from its skin. Then I looked. I saw that lover, Beloved, and love are one because in that state of unification all can be one.

– Bāyazīd al-Bisṭāmī [FAD/ES250]

Unification (*tawḥīd*) is defined as "the absoluteness of the Divine nature realized in the passing away of the human nature," so that "the man's last state reverts to his first state and he becomes even as he was before he existed."

– Abū Naṣr as-Sarrāj [NIC/IP13]

With God, two I's cannot find room. You say "I" and He says "I." Either you die before Him, or let Him die before you; then duality will not remain. But it is impossible for Him to die, either subjectively or objectively, since He is *the Living God, the Undying* (25:58). He possesses such Gentleness that were it possible, He would die for you so that duality might vanish. But since it is impossible for Him to die, you die, so that He may manifest Himself to you and duality may vanish.

– Jalāl ad-Dīn Rūmī [CHI/PL191]

Everything perishes except His Face (28:88). It is not that it perishes at some particular moment, but rather it is forever perishing, since it cannot be conceived except as perishing. For each thing other than God is, when considered in and by itself, pure nothingness; and if considered from the Face to which existence flows to it from the Prime Reality, it is viewed as existing, but not in itself, solely from *the Face* which accompanies Him Who gives it existence. Therefore, the Divine Face is the sole thing in reality.

– Abū Ḥāmid al-Ghazālī [KAZ/JR176]

Another group, who are the elect of the elect, pass beyond this. The august glories of His Face burn them up, and the ruling authority of majesty overcomes them. In their essences they are effaced and annihilated. They become extinct from themselves, so that they cease observing themselves. Nothing remains save the One, the Real. The meaning of His words, *Everything is perishing except His Face* (28:88), becomes for them a taste and a state. This is the ultimate end of those who have arrived.

– Abū Ḥāmid al-Ghazālī [BUC/NL52]

Now he knows the meaning of *Everything is perishing but its face* (28:88), and he will know why the pronoun "its" here must refer to "everything"; because everything perishes in its form but subsists in its meaning, its "face." He will grasp that in one respect this "face" is the Self-Manifestation of God; for *The face of thy Lord remains* (55:27). Dear reader, when you yourself have realized that the meaning and reality of things is identical with this Divine Countenance, you will pray, "Show us things as they are" (*ḥadīth*) and by this come to see with inward vision that

> in everything there is a sign
> a clue to "He is One."

Say "Whose is the earth and whoso is in it, if you have knowledge?" They will say "God's" (23:86). Verily we belong to Him and subsist through Him.

– Fakhr ad-Dīn 'Irāqī [CHI/DF126]

Anybody who has come to terms with himself and accepted his self is dead, even though he appears to be alive. Whoever lives in God, however, even though he appears to be dead, is really alive. Death is not the death of the body! Nonexistence is not the nonexistence of the body! Just as there is an apparent death, there is also a real one. Men are sunk in the sea of human nature. The prophets come along and, through their assistance, men are extricated from their plight. They then become submerged in the ocean of Unity, till not a trace from even one of them is left behind!

O brother, when the sun of Unity rises, certainly the lamp of your being, out of modesty, will flicker into nothingness! You will continue to exist since it is only with respect to appearances that you will be nothing. A lamp, face to face with the sun, for instance, would have no brilliance of itself: All brightness would stem from the sun. Since no effect flows from its presence, its existence would be tantamount to nonexistence.

– Sharaf ad-Dīn Manīrī [JAC/HL353]

God—may He be exalted!—said to me, "Do you know who you are?" I replied, "Yes, I am the non-being which is manifested by Your manifestation; I am the darkness which Your light illuminates."

Then He said to me, "Since you know this, persevere firmly [in this knowledge] and be careful not to claim that which does not belong to you: for the deposit (*amāna*) must be returned to its owner and the loan must be paid back. The name 'contingent being' has always belonged to you and always will belong to you."

He said to me again, "Do you know who you are?" I replied, "Yes, I am in reality God (*al-Ḥaqq*) [the Real]. But, metaphorically and in relation to the Way, I am creature (*al-khalq*). I am a contingent being with respect to my form, but I cannot not be the necessary Being. It is the divine name *al-Ḥaqq* which belongs to me by original right; the name of creature is only a borrowed name and a formula of differentiation."

He said to me, "Veil this symbol; and let the wall fall down and bury this treasure, in order that only he will be able to extract it who has put his soul through severe trials and looked his death in the face."

– Amir 'Abd al-Qādir al-Jazā'irī [CHO/AK77-78]

Fanā' and the Self

Foundational Sources

And when they saw him, they extolled him, and cut their hands [distracted from themselves by Joseph's beauty].
– Qur'ān 12:31

What is with you must vanish; what is with God will endure.
– Qur'ān 16:96

Sufi Aphorisms

Leave aside your self and come!
– Bāyazīd al-Bisṭāmī [CHI/PK438]

May God empty my very self of all except His own presence.
– Anonymous [VAU/TP185]

The finding (*wujūd*) of the Real occurs though the loss of your self.
– Abū'l-Qāsim al-Junayd [SEL/EI131]

Take one step outside yourself: the whole Path lasts no longer than a step.
– Shāh Ni'matullāh Walī [WIL/DU30]

Annihilation is that you become totally ignorant of your own attributes and totally occupied with His Totality.
– Abū'l-Qāsim al-Junayd [NUR/SF111]

An hour reflecting on one's own nonexistence is better than a year of religious devotions with the thought that one exists.
– Abū Sa'īd Ibn Abī'l-Khayr [OKA/SG53]

Sufi Poetry

Neither am I aware of being a lover, nor of love,
Neither of my self, nor of the Beloved.
– Aḥmad al-Ghazālī [POU/SI66]

Between me and You there lingers an "it is I"
which torments me.
Ah! lift through mercy this "it is I"
from between us both!
– Ḥusayn Ibn Manṣūr al-Ḥallāj [MAS/3P47]

What you most want,
what you travel around wishing to find,
lose yourself as lovers lose themselves,
and you'll *be* that.

– Farīd ad-Dīn 'Aṭṭār [KHA/HP75]

I saw the Friend in my dream and I asked,
"Which path will lead me to you?"
He declared, "You'll find me when you
abandon you."

– Ḥajjī Bektāsh Walī [FER/QGxxiv]

In the empty heart, void of self
Can be heard the echoing cry,
"I am the Truth."
Thus is man one with the Eternal,
Traveling, travel, and traveler have become one.

– Sa'd ad-Dīn Maḥmūd Shabistarī [LED/SR60]

A man of perfection
walked the path of annihilation
and departed from existence
like dust.
A thread of his being
went along with him—
in poverty's eye,
that thread was an infidel's belt.

– Naṣīr ad-Dīn Qūnawī [CHI/FP144]

O desire
of the desirous,
Take me from myself
to Thyself!
Love for Thee took away
my we-ness and I-ness—
Thy love leaves
no choice but selflessness

– Naṣīr ad-Dīn Qūnawī [CHI/FP91]

My friend, everything existing
exists through Him;
your own existence is a mere pretence.

No more nonsense! Lose yourself,
and the hell of your heart becomes a heaven.
Lose yourself, and anything can be accomplished.
– Hakim Sanā'ī [PEN/WG19]

When annihilation adorns a man because of his poverty,
he becomes shadowless, like Muḥammad.
Annihilation was the adornment of him who said,
"Poverty is my pride."
Like the flame of a candle, he had no shadow.
When the candle is wholly annihilated in the fire,
you will see no trace of it or its flames.
– Jalāl ad-Dīn Rūmī [CHI/PL188]

Pass away—
then you'll find
the eternal shore.
To reach the Friend,
you have to go beyond yourself.

One day a bubble
was wondering
about its existence—

When it popped,
it finally
rejoined
the sea.
– Fikrī Khurāsānī [FID/LA78]

How can Time know my name and trace?
Who but the Friend could know my essence and attribute?
When someone's existence has been concealed by God,
how can he be known by any but Him?
I who am lost in Thee—how could anyone find me?
Who on the shore knows the one drowned in Thy Sea?
I who am not light—how should the men of Light know me?
I who am not fire—how should the men of Fire know me?
Since I have packed my bags and left both worlds,
how can I be considered one of those who must
settle accounts on the Day of Resurrection?
I who have lost my being in Thee—no being knows me.

I am drunk in Thee—how could a sober man know me?
Speak not of the many before me—who has seen the One.
How can he who has seen only the One know the many?
He who is shackled by heart, spirit, intellect, and soul—
how could he know me, me who has escaped from all four?
How can the one imprisoned in the dungeon of created being
have news of Maghribī, who has fled the dungeon? How?

– Shams ad-Dīn al-Maghribī [NUR/SF114]

Sufi Instruction

Know that when you learn to lose yourself, you will reach the Beloved. There is no other secret to be learned, and more than this is not known to me.

– Khwāja 'Abd Allāh Anṣārī [VAU/TP188]

Go you, sweep out the dwelling-room of your heart, prepare it to be the abode and home of the Beloved: when you go out He will come in. Within you, when you are free from self, He will show His Beauty.

– Sa'd ud-Dīn Maḥmūd Shabistarī [BHA/DC118]

When peace in the heart reaches its utmost limit, naturally the Sufi no longer looks at his own essence. His awareness of his own selfhood is nullified. This is called the "greatest annihilation." And when he forgets himself and forgets even his forgetfulness, this is called "annihilation within annihilation."

– Shihāb ad-Dīn Suhrawardī [NUR/SF89]

A hundred spiritual masters have spoken concerning Sufism. The first said the same as the last. The modes of expression were different but the meaning was one: "Sufism is dropping all affectation." And there is no affectation that comes before your own you-ness. The moment you become involved with your own self, you are cut off from Him.

– Abū Sa'īd Ibn Abī'l-Khayr [OKA/SG308]

The people of perfection have realized all stations and states and passed beyond these to the station above both majesty and beauty, so they have no attribute and no description. It was said to Bāyazīd, "How are you this morning?" He replied, "I have no morning and no evening; morning and evening belong to him who becomes delimited by attributes, and I have no attributes."

– Muḥyī ad-Dīn Ibn al-'Arabī [CHI/PK376]

Do not say "I" before having been extinguished [in God]. You will have no life before having undergone death. The suns will not rise in you until after the death of the souls. You will not reach the goal you desire so long as people still have praises for you. You will not taste the food of faith until you come out from the created worlds. You will reach extinction (*fanā'*) only after having died to the evanescent world. If the veils were to be torn asunder for you, you would contemplate the Beloved in yourself. If the suggestions of imagination were to cease, you would contemplate the eternal without ceasing. If your soul did not take you away from Him, you would see no reality except your Lord. If your soul were freed of filth, the Truth would come and vanity would disappear.[3]

– Mulay al-'Arabī ad-Darqāwī [BUR/LS24]

He is like one dumbfounded, absorbed in the sea of the direct witnessing, whose inner state resembles that of the ladies who cut their hands, witnessing the beauty of Joseph, when they were dumbfounded and their perceptions were gone.[4] The Sufis express this state by saying that "he has passed away from himself." Whenever a man has passed away from himself, he has passed away from all besides himself. Then it is as if he passed away from everything except the Witnessed One, and passed away from the act of witnessing. For the heart, whenever it turns aside to view the act of witnessing and itself as a witness, becomes heedless of the Witnessed One. And for he who is infatuated with a thing which he sees, there is no turning aside, in his state of absorption, toward his witnessing, nor toward his own self through which his vision comes, nor toward his heart in which his joy lies.

– Abū Ḥāmid al-Ghazālī [NAK/ISxxvii]

[3] See Qur'ān (17:81): "And say: 'The truth has come, and falsehood has vanished away; surely falsehood is ever certain to vanish.'"

[4] An allusion to the Qur'ānic story of Joseph. See Qur'ān (12:30-31): "Certain women that were in the city said, 'The Governor's wife is seeking to seduce her servant; he smote her heart with love; we see her in manifest error.' When she heard their sly whispers, she sent to them, and made ready for them a repast, then she gave to each one of them a knife. 'Come forth, attend to them,' she said. And when they saw him, they so admired him that they cut their hands, saying, 'God save us! This is no mortal; he is no other but a noble angel.'"

From *Fanā'* to *Baqā'*

Foundational Sources

All that dwells upon the earth is perishing, yet still abides the Face of your Lord, majestic, splendid.

– Qur'ān 55:26

And you [O Muḥammad] did not throw when you threw, but God threw.

– Qur'ān 8:17

Sufi Aphorisms

When poverty is perfect, God appears.

– Sharaf ad-Dīn Manīrī [JAC/QG202]

Eternal permanence [with God] is in your annihilation of your self.

– Abū Madyan [COR/AM136]

The right to eternal permanence is in your annihilation of self.

– Abū Madyan [COR/AM144]

When He is there, thou art not, and if thou art there, He is not.

– Abū'l-Qāsim al-Junayd [KAZ/OL127]

Subsistence belongs to the Real, extinction to what is not Him.

– Abū'l-Qāsim al-Junayd [LOZ/AM362]

When the devotee is annihilated in terms of his own attributes, he finds perfect subsistence.

– Abū'l-Qāsim al-Junayd [ERN/WE28]

I went from God to God, until He cried from me in me, "O Thou I." Thus I attained the stage of annihilation in God.

– Bāyazīd al-Bisṭāmī [BHA/DC59]

Here is the candle extinguished and there the living light of the Sun! Mark the difference between the one and the other!

– Muḥammad Shams ad-Dīn Ḥāfiẓ [VAL/QS15]

He who knows himself as nothingness, knows his Lord as Being.[5]

– Abū Sa'īd Ibn Abī'l-Khayr [NUR/2T45]

[5] This is an allusion and comment upon the well known *ḥadīth*, "He who knows himself, knows his Lord."

Sufi Poetry

Come into the garden of annihilation and behold:
paradise after paradise within the spirit of your own subsistence.
– Jalāl ad-Dīn Rūmī [CHI/PL179]

After extinction I came out and I
Eternal now am, though not as I,
Yet who am I, O I, but I?
– Abū'l-Ḥasan ash-Shushtarī [LIN/WS88]

My hearing, sight, my tongue and hand: all He.
Then I am not, for all that is, is He.
I think I am, and thought is but a dream.
When I awake, all that remains is He.
– Bābā Afzal Kāshāni [WIL/DU29]

Some people wander in a desert wilderness,
While others wander in the land of His love.
They are annihilated, then annihilated
then annihilated,
Yet they are preserved in permanence
through the nearness of His nearness.
– Ibn 'Aṭā' Allāh al-Iskandarī [ROB/SB39]

Once again we have left our heart, intellect, and spirit behind—
the Friend has come into the midst and we have disappeared.
We have turned back from annihilation and become woven into
subsistence;
we have found the Traceless and thrown away all traces.
– Jalāl ad-Dīn Rūmī [CHI/PL180]

In my annihilation, my annihilation
was annihilated,
And in my annihilation,
I found Thee.
Thou obliterated my name and the trace
of my body;
I was asked about myself
and said "Thou."
– Abū'l-Hasan 'Alī al-Hujwīrī [NUR/SF106]

A mystic is one
who passes away—

He abides in the essence
of that which is Real.

Such a person is pure,
clear wine without dregs.

Now whole, he displays
the Most Beautiful Names.

– Binavi Badakhshanī [FID/LA171]

I became water
    and saw myself
        a mirage
became an ocean
    saw myself a speck
        of foam
gained Awareness
    saw that all is but
        forgetfulness
woke up
    and found myself
        asleep.

– Binavi Badakhshanī [WIL/DU95]

If you could get rid
Of yourself just once,
The secret of secrets
Would open to you.
The face of the unknown,
Hidden beyond the universe
Would appear on the
Mirror of your perception.

– Jalāl ad-Dīn Rūmī [FAD/ES244]

The heart enquired of the soul
What is the beginning of this business?
What its end, and what its fruit?
The soul answered:
The beginning of it is
the annihilation of self,

Its end faithfulness,
And its fruit immortality.
– Khwāja 'Abd Allāh Anṣārī [NAS/SE34]

For someone whose trade is emptiness
and whose work is annihilation,
the search for certainty, knowledge,
and religion
has come to an end.

Since he's annihilated,
only God remains—
just God.

This is the meaning of
"when poverty becomes complete,
you find God."
– Abū Sa'īd Ibn Abī'l-Khayr [FID/LA142]

Love came
    flowed like blood
        beneath skin, through veins
emptied me of my self
    filled me
        with the Beloved
till every limb
    every organ was seized
        and occupied
till only
    my name remains,
        the rest is It.
– Abū Sa'īd Ibn Abī'l-Khayr [WIL/DU101]

The seeker of the Court of God's like this:
When God appears, the seeker fades away.
Yes, this encounter brings eternal life,
but effacement comes before undying life.
Could shadows, say, be seekers of the light?
When the light shines, the shadows disappear.
How could reason live when sacrificed to Him?
All but His Face shall perish from the earth (28:88).
Being and nothing fade before His Face;
What a miracle, to be in nothingness!

In these precincts wisdom and logic fail
and at this point, the pen is split in two.
– Jalāl ad-Dīn Rūmī [LEW/SS117]

Sufi Instruction

Subsistence is a relationship that does not disappear or change. Its property is immutably fixed in both the Real and the creature. It is a divine attribute. But annihilation is a relationship that disappears. It is an attribute of engendered existence and does not touch upon the Presence of the Real.

– Muḥyī ad-Dīn Ibn al-'Arabī [CHI/PK321]

The saint is the one who is annihilated in his state, while God is present in his witnessing of the Real; God takes responsibility for his governing, and the lights of authority come upon him continually. He has no information about himself, nor reliance on any other than God.

– Abū 'Alī al-Juzjānī [ERN/SG60]

Self-annihilation consists in this, that through the overpowering influence of the Very Being upon the inner man, there remains no consciousness of aught besides Him. Annihilation of annihilation consists in this, that there remains no consciousness even of that unconsciousness. It is evident that annihilation of annihilation is involved in annihilation.

– 'Abd ar-Raḥmān Jāmī [BHA/DC132]

I was in three states. I was in one state in which, if everything in heaven and earth wept for me on account of my bewilderment, it would be no wonder. I was in another state in which, if I wept for everything in heaven and earth on account of their hiddenness from God and their striving with Him, it would be no wonder. I was in another state in which I saw nothing but the quality of eternity and might and will and dominion and decree. I contemplated primordiality and finality. Then I became hidden from the all, and annihilated from the all, and I became subsistent in the all.

– Abū'l-Qāsim al-Junayd [ERN/WE28]

Being wholly present in God, he is wholly lost to self. And thus he is present before God, absent in himself; absent and present at the same time. He is where he is not and he is not where he is. Then after he has not been, he is where he is [before creation]. He is himself, after he has not been truly himself. He is existent in himself and existent in God after having been existent in God and non-existent in himself. This is because he has left the drunkenness of God's overwhelming and come to the clarity of sobriety, and contemplation is once more restored to him, so that he can put everything in its right place and assess it correctly.

– Abū'l-Qāsim al-Junayd [KAD/AJ172]

It surely behoves you to make an effort and to turn away from self, and turn your face towards the Absolute Reality, and concern yourself with Him, Who is the Creative Truth. You must know that created things, in their different types, are all of them means whereby His Beauty is manifested, and the diverse classes of creatures are all mirrors which reflect His perfection. You must continue to strive in this way, until He dwells in your soul and your own existence passes out of your sight, and if you regard yourself, you are regarding Him, and when you say anything of yourself, you say it of Him. That which was finite has become infinite and "I am the Truth" is the same as "He is the Truth."

– 'Abd ar-Raḥmān Jāmī [SMI/RM86]

You must strive so that dispersed thoughts strike their tents outside the breast's courtyard and the light of the Real Being's manifestation—glory be to Him!—casts its rays on your nonmanifest realm. It will take you away from you and free you from the jostling of the others. No consciousness of yourself will remain, nor any consciousness of the self's lack of consciousness. Rather, nothing will subsist but God, the One, the Unitary.

O Lord, help—so that I may escape from my own animality,
so that I may cut myself off from the bad and escape
from my own evil!
Take my self away from myself in Your own Being
so that I may escape my selfhood and selflessness.

– 'Abd ar-Raḥmān Jāmī [MUR/CG146]

Subsistence is your relationship with the Real. . . . But annihilation is your relationship with the engendered universe, since you say, "I have been annihilated from such and such." Your relationship to the Real is higher. Hence subsistence is a higher relationship, since the two are interrelated states.

None subsists in this path except him who is annihilated, and none is annihilated except him who subsists. The one described by annihilation will always be in the state of subsistence, and the one described by subsistence will always be in the state of annihilation.

In the relationship of subsistence is the witnessing of the Real, while in the relationship of annihilation is the witnessing of creation. You cannot say, "I was annihilated from such and such," without conceiving of what you were annihilated from. Your very conception of that is your witnessing it, since you cannot avoid making it present to yourself in order to conceive of the property of becoming annihilated from it.

Subsistence is the same. You must witness the one through whom you subsist, and in this path, subsistence is only through the Real. Hence you have to witness the Real, since you must have made Him present in your heart and conceived of Him. Then you will say, "I subsist through the Real." This relationship is nobler and higher, because of the highness of the one with whom it is established. Hence the state of subsistence is higher than the state of annihilation, even if the two necessitate each other and are found in a single person at the same time.

– Muḥyī ad-Dīn Ibn al-'Arabī [CHI/IW61-62]

Baqā' and the Divine Presence

Foundational Sources

God is better and more abiding.

– Qur'ān 20:73

He is the Hearing, the Seeing.

– Qur'ān 42:11

My servant draws near to me by nothing dearer than that which I have established as a duty for him. And My servant does not cease to approach Me through supererogatory acts until I love him. And when I love him, I become his hearing with which he hears, his sight with which he sees, his hand with which he grasps, and his foot with which he walks.

– *Ḥadīth Qudsī* [HIR/DS88]

Make me into a light.[6]

– *Ḥadīth* [CHI/SD438]

[6] This is the final line of the famous "Light Prayer" of the Prophet: "O God, place in my heart a light, in my hearing a light, in my eyesight a light, on my right hand a light, on my left hand a light, before me a light, behind me a light, above me a light, below me a light, and make me into a light" (trans. Sachiko Murata). It in turn may best be grasped in its significance in relation to the famous "Light Verse" of the Qur'ān, asserting the identification of light with the Divine, which begins "God is the Light of the heavens and the earth" (24:35).

I am the time of times, I am the cause of causes, I am the face of God toward which you turn, I am the side of God on which you rely. I come from God into a place, but when I am pious, then I am He.

– 'Alī ibn Abī Ṭālib [ERN/WE23]

I am the Sign of the All-Powerful. I am the gnosis of the mysteries. I am the Threshold of Thresholds. I am the companion of the radiance of the divine Majesty. I am the First and the Last, the Manifest and the Hidden. I am the Face of God. I am the mirror of God, the Supreme Pen, the Preserved Tablet. I am he who in the Gospel is called Elijah. I am he who is in possession of the secret of God's Messenger.

– 'Alī ibn Abī Ṭālib [KAZ/JR187]

Sufi Aphorisms

They move as God causes them to move, and their words are the words of God which roll upon their tongues, and their sight is the sight of God which has entered their eyes.

– Dhū'l Nūn al-Misrī [NIC/MI79]

God—nothing else: attachments severed, secondary causes dissolved, appearances nullified, limitations naughted, understandings annihilated, history absurd, allusions blind, expressions negated, harm obliterated, and God the One subsists through His own Selfhood.

– Khwāja 'Abd Allāh Anṣārī [NUR/SF113]

Sufi Poetry

I am plunged in the Light like the sun;
I cannot distinguish myself from the light.

– Jalāl ad-Dīn Rūmī [VAL/CD160]

The secret that is in your heart is not a sermon—
you can say it on the gallows, but not in the pulpit!

– Mīrzā Ghālib [SCH/TC126]

Who is the one hearing my voice in my ear?
Who is the one who pronounces the words in my mouth?
Who is the one in my eyes, borrowing my sight?
Who is the soul whose clothing I am?

– Jalāl ad-Dīn Rūmī [VIT/RS135]

He am I whom I love, He whom I love is I,
Two Spirits in one single body dwelling.
So seest thou me, then seest thou Him,
And seest thou Him, then seest thou Us.

– Ḥusayn Ibn Manṣūr al-Ḥallāj [LIN/SP38]

I am God, I am creature;
  I am Lord, I am servant.
I am the Throne and the mat one treads on;
  I am hell and I am the blissful eternity.
I am water, I am fire;
  I am air and the earth.
I am the "how much" and the "how";
  I am the presence and the absence.
I am the essence and the attributes;
  I am the near and the far.
All being is my being;
  I am the Only, I am the Unique.

– Amir 'Abd al-Qādir al-Jazā'irī [CHO/AK181]

I saw my Lord with the eye of my heart, so I asked,
  Who are you? He said, You.
And there is no "where" apart from you,
  and no "where" where you are.
Imagination can conceive no image of you,
  so how can imagination know where you are?
You are the One that encompasses every "where"
  on the way to "no where," so where are you?
So in my passing away even my dying to self has vanished,
  and in my loss of self you are found.

– Ḥusayn Ibn Manṣūr al-Ḥallāj [REN/SD111]

When Bāyazīd said, "Glory unto me!"
he did not speak in ignorance or folly;
and the tongue that uttered that final secret
moved truly when announcing, "I am God."
When Ḥallāj tried to teach the back
the secret that the face had taught him,
it turned hangman and destroyed him;
his secret's daylight then became pitch darkness.
Yet it was God's own word that he spoke;
and when in the crowd he suddenly disclosed

the forbidden secret, his outer form
was given to the gallows; but the friend
took his inner being to himself;
and when his life could speak no more,
his heart's blood still disclosed the secret.
– Hakim Sanā'ī [PEN/WG29]

I am the first and the last; I am the soul to the souls.
I am the one who brings ready aid
to those stranded on the Way.
I became stable.
Who can perceive my secret?
How will the one without eyes see me?
I am the one who hid in the heart.
I am the one who became a drop at the moment of "Be!"[7]
who arranged the world at one look.
I am the one who arranged the feast table
through exceptional power;
I am the one who strikes the kettle drum of love.
I laid out these places flat; I nailed in these mountains.
I made the sky into shades;
it is I who grasp and roll it up again. . . .
It is not Yūnus who is saying this; it is his Self saying this.
He who doesn't believe this is a misbeliever:
I am the Beginning and the End.
– Yūnus Emre [SMI/PY94]

Sufi Instruction

But the Essence of God may be seen only through God and this experience takes "the man" out of a man, rendering him selfless. This is the meaning of the first part of the verse *Vision comprehends Him not* (6:103)—which ravishes the wayfarer from himself—but the second part *but He comprehends all Vision* (6:103) implies that all is God.
– 'Ayn al-Quḍāt Hamadhānī [LEW/WS204]

The mighty and glorious Lord has men who stand entirely through Him, who move and rest entirely through Him, who live through Him, and who abide through the contemplation of Him. If they stop contemplating the Real for even one moment, their souls fly from

[7] This is in reference to the Qur'ānic passage regarding the act of Divine creation: "It is He who created the heavens and the earth in truth; and the day He says 'Be!', and it is (*kun fayakūn*)" (6:73).

them. They sleep through Him, they eat through Him, they take through Him, they walk through Him, they see through Him, they hear through Him, they exist through Him.

– Abū'l-Ḥusayn an-Nūrī [LOZ/AM370]

Annihilation is the end of the journey to God, while subsistence is the beginning of the journey in God—for the journey to God comes to an end when the traveler traverses totally the desert of existence on the feet of sincerity, while the journey in God becomes actualized when, after absolute annihilation, the servant is given an existence and essence cleansed from the stain of temporality. By means of this existence and essence, he ascends within the world of becoming qualified by the Divine Attributes and acquiring the Divine Traits.

– 'Izz ad-Dīn Kāshāni [NUR/SF107]

When the mystery—of realizing that the mystic is one with the Divine—is revealed to you, you will understand that you are no other than God and that you have continued and will continue . . . without when and without times. Then you will see all your actions to be His actions and all your attributes to be His attributes and your essence to be His essence, though you do not thereby become He or He you, in either the greatest or the least degree. *Everything is perishing save His Face* (28:88), that is, there is nothing except His Face, then *whithersoever you turn, there is the Face of God* (2:115).

– Muḥyī ad-Dīn Ibn al-'Arabī [BHA/DC92]

The Sufi becomes more humble every hour, for every hour is drawing him nearer to God. The Sufis see without knowledge, without sight, without information received, and without observation, without description, without veiling and without veil. They are not themselves, but insofar as they exist at all, they exist in God. Their movements are caused by God, and their words are the words of God uttered by their tongues, and their sight is the sight of God, which has entered into their eyes. So God Most High has said, *When I love a servant, I, the Lord, am his ear so that he hears by Me, I am his eye so that he sees by Me, and I am his tongue so that he speaks by Me, and I am his hand so that he takes by Me* (*ḥadīth qudsī*).

– Dhū'l Nūn al-Misrī [SCH/MD43]

Love means that the attributes of the lover are changed into those of the Beloved. Now he lives in accordance with the saying of God: *When I love him, I will be his eye by which he sees and his hearing by which he hears and his hand by which he reaches out* (*ḥadīth qudsī*)

. . . for the saint is submerged in the ocean of Unity, by passing away from himself and from the demands of the creatures upon himself and from all response to them, into the realization of the Unicity of God, into the direct experience of His Presence. He leaves behind him his own feelings and actions, as he passes into the life with God, and so becomes that which God desired for him, that the servant, at the last, should return to the state in which he was at first, and should become as he was before he began to be.

– Abū'l-Qāsim al-Junayd [SMI/RM21]

If God Most Glorious manifests His Essence to anyone, that one will find all his own essence and attributes and actions utterly absorbed in the light of God's Essence and the Divine qualities and actions and will; and he sees his essence to be the Essence of the One, and his attributes to be the attributes of God, and his actions to be God's actions, because of his complete absorption in Union with the Divine; and beyond this stage, there is no further stage of union for man. For when the eye of the soul—the spiritual vision—is rapt away to the contemplation of the Divine Beauty, the light of the understanding, whereby we distinguish between things, is extinguished in the dazzling light of the Eternal Essence, and the distinction between the temporal and the eternal, the perishable and the imperishable, is taken away, and this state is called "Union."

– 'Abd ar-Raḥmān Jāmī [SMI/SE217]

In the deep waters of the ocean of annihilation I would seek to be, for though I aspire to the Sun, yet, since one is powerless to attain to Your great height, I would aspire to sleep at Your feet. Behold what grief I suffer without You! But now, since I have become nothing, I know that in the end I shall attain again to my desire. I said unto You: "I have passed away, as I was asked to do." You said to me: "I will bring you to Eternal Life, as you have wished, for when you see yourself as nothing, then will I give to you such an existence as you have desired."

Every moment now I spend in loving adoration of Another than myself. Long ago I died to my own existence and if now I live, it is in the existence of Another. I sacrificed all tranquility and ease and renounced all hope of fame, so that I might attain to complete annihilation. I laid down my life and sacrificed my soul, and all mankind became as nothing to me. Now I have arisen, and I am free from all grief of soul, for I am set free from the world of Existence and Non-Existence and I dwell beyond both. I have taken my flight from phenomenal existence to non-entity.

– Farīd ad-Dīn 'Aṭṭār [SMI/RM60]

VI. Concuding Essay: The *Shahādah* and the Path of Unity

The *Shahādah* and the Human Situation

Man, endowed with reason, is by nature a thinking being. In light of this, every tradition has recognized that the formation of man's thought—in terms of appropriate content, manner, and concentration—is a matter of immense, even central, importance. A fundamental insight of the great sapiential traditions is that man's reason is insufficient of itself to address issues of transcendent concern, but rather must be informed by either revelation or intellection. In this way, a tradition teaches man how to "think rightly"; hence the emphasis of religions upon orthodoxy, from the Greek *orthodoxos*—having right thought or correct opinion. In a profound sense, the very purpose of the sapiential traditions is to convey sacred truths to man so that his thought and being might be shaped in light of those truths.

In Islam, the central truths of the Qur'ānic revelation are Unity and Mercy. These two great themes, which both dominate and permeate the Islamic tradition, are given their most concise expression in the *Shahādah*, the two statements that form the Islamic testification of faith. In reciting the *Shahādah*, the Muslim bears witness that "There is no god but God" (*lā ilāha illā 'Llāh*) and that "Muḥammad is the messenger of God" (*Muḥammadun rasūlu 'Llāh*).

The first statement of faith—termed the *tahlīl*, first *kalimah*, or first *Shahādah*—describes the nature of reality as such, dominated by an essential Unity, by God as the sole deity. The Arabic word for God, *Allāh*,[1] does not signify a deity with particular characteristics or for a particular people; etymologically it simply means "the God." The name *Allāh* is particular to Arabic, but not particular to Islam; Yemeni Jews and Syriac Christians—who speak Arabic as their native tongue—have prayed to God as *Allāh* for centuries. In addition, the Qur'ān is explicit that Allah is not a deity particular to either Arabs or Muslims, but is the One God, the God of Abraham, Moses, Jesus, and of all peoples.

[1] In what follows, "Allah" has been employed to refer to God as such in an Islamic context, while "*Allāh*" has been employed to refer to the specific Arabic denotation of God. The first usage refers to the Divinity, the second usage to the *name* of the Divinity.

The second statement of faith—the second *kalimah* or second *Shahādah*—illustrates God's essential Mercy, identifying Muḥammad as the bearer of Divine guidance for the Islamic community. Here, there is no implication that Muḥammad is the sole prophet, or messenger, of God; rather, the Qur'ān insists upon the universality of prophethood and upon the essential equivalence between prophets.

Given the primacy of thought in establishing the nature of man's volitive and active life, the nature and content of his thought essentially determines man; if he is purified or corrupted, he is so first in his thoughts. In the most basic sense, man *is* his thought; it is his thought that impels both his character and condition. As Jalāl al-Dīn Rūmī reminds us:

> Brother, you are this very thought—
> the rest of you is bones and fiber.
> If roses are your thought, you are a rose garden,
> if thorns, you are fuel for the furnace.
> If rosewater, you will be sprinkled on the neck,
> if urine, you will be dumped in a hole.[2]

In this respect, the human being faces a double challenge: not only does reason in isolation lack intrinsic guidance with respect to matters of ultimate concern, but there are other forces—most notably passion and distraction—that are operative within man. The Qur'ān characterizes these typical mental tendencies by the words heedlessness (*ghafla*) and forgetfulness (*nisyān*); in this, it recognizes that the fundamental problem of man is at root a problem of thought—of consciousness, attention, and awareness.

To the degree that man's thought fails to conform to reality, to the degree that his mental tendencies render him insensate both to his true nature and vocation as well as to God, to that degree he is characterized by both heedlessness and forgetfulness. Man's attention is too often both circumscribed by the circle of his limited preoccupations and scattered outward in attraction to the phenomenal world. He is dominated by habits and passions that dull his intellect and disperse his will. Heedlessness and forgetfulness, far from being isolated in their significance, affect the whole of man. In a sense, these tendencies arise from the inherent multiplicity that man is immersed in; the very nature of the phenomenal world—its multifaceted glamour—bears the potentiality of leading man toward passional dispersion.

[2] *Mathnawi* (R. A. Nicholson edition), II, 277-279, trans. William C. Chittick; on this theme, see also William C. Chittick, "The Rehabilitation of Islamic Thought," *Iqbal Review* 41:4 (2000).

Unity and the Adequation of Intelligence

In the face of the undirectedness of reason and the heedlessness and forgetfulness of passional dispersion, the *Shahādah* serves to orient thought in harmony with the nature of the Real. The inherent content of the *Shahādah* serves as an integrative center for mental understanding, grounding man in the verities of his situation, acting as an anchor of certainty against confusion or dissipation. In a sense, forgetfulness and heedlessness represent a failure of thought; in this sense also, the inculcation of the *Shahādah* and its concomitant ramifications represent thought brought to its proper consummation.

The first *Shahādah*—"There is no god but God" (*lā ilāha illā 'Llāh*)—is a succinct summary of essential truth to which human thought may be conformed. Its words vehicle a meaning that is homologous to the most fundamental nature of reality, and these words, in their brevity, depth, precision, density, and synthesis, have the capability of impacting their meaning upon human awareness, consciousness, mental structures, and habits of thought in such a way as to effect human transformation.

Although man stands in need of the truth of Unity as expressed in the first *Shahādah*, it is a truth for which he already bears an inherent intuition. This fundamental truth of Unity—termed *tawḥīd* in the Islamic tradition—is in a sense self-evident: it stands behind our expectations that the world is ordered and not chaotic, that it is comprehensible and not incoherent; it lies at the root of both our innate convictions and our formal sciences. This inherent intuition of Unity not only serves to confirm the truth of *tawḥīd*, but also indicates the adequation of man's intelligence to the comprehension of the essential nature of the Real. Further, the very fact that the fundamental truth of Unity is taught to man in the first *Shahādah* implies that man's intelligence is adequate to grasp this truth:

> The real nature of intelligence is ultimately to come to realize that *lā ilāha illā 'Llāh*, that is to come to know that in the end there is only one Absolute Reality. It is to realize the absolute nature of Allah and the relativity of all else that is other than He. Moreover, it is only this truth which the intelligence can know in an absolute sense.[3]

This adequation is necessarily predicated on the essential conformity of the human substance to reality, a conformity indicated in the

[3] Seyyed Hossein Nasr, *Ideals and Realities of Islam* (London: Unwin Hyman, 1979), p. 19.

Prophetic *ḥadīth*, "He who knows himself knows his Lord." Thus the first *Shahādah* is in essence a reminder of what is already grasped by the innate human intellect, namely the truth of *tawḥīd*.

The Shahādah as Viaticum

In Latin, the word *viaticum* refers at once to the provisions for a journey as well as to the Eucharist, or Word of God, particularly when given in danger of death. In an analogous sense, the *Shahādah* may be considered as a *viaticum*, as at once provision and Word. Thus, the second *Shahādah*, essentializing Prophetic guidance in the context of the Divine Mercy, is provision for man's spiritual life; the first *Shahādah*, essentializing the Divine Unity and containing the Divine Name, presents the Word to man. Alternatively, the *Shahadah* as a whole is at once provision and Word; indeed, the very provision of the *Shahādah* is in the Word and words that it bears.

Together, the two *Shahādah*s convey in essence what is of greatest import for man: the oneness of God and the reality of Divine guidance. In addition, the return of man to God is implicit in the statement of Divine unicity, while the proper modality of that return is implicit in the statement of Divine guidance. In this sense, the *Shahādah*—in its witnessing—is not only the most fundamental ritual act, but also serves as a summary statement encompassing the three domains of Islamic faith: oneness, prophethood, and the return to God. This centrality of the *Shahādah* for both activity and faith is attested to in the saying of the Prophet, "I have brought nothing more important than the *Shahādah*."

While the *Shahādah* essentializes both right activity and right faith, it also temporally encompasses and pervades the life of the Muslim. The first words that the child of Muslim parents will hear upon being born are those of the *Shahādah*, whispered as part of the call to prayer into his ear. The first words that a convert to Islam will say, the very words that mark his entry into the community, are those of the *Shahādah*, spoken before witnesses. The last words that a dying Muslim will speak on his deathbed are those of the *Shahādah*, reciting them repeatedly as he awaits his return to God. Five times each day, the *Shahādah* is called out from the minarets as part of the call to prayer, and is recited by every Muslim as part of the ritual prayer. The first *Shahādah* is often recited continually, either silently or aloud, both by Sufis and by other Muslims as a means of sustaining the remembrance of God.

The first *Shahādah* permeates the temporal experience of Muslim life, but it is radically atemporal in content, evoking a sense of timelessness and eternality. For man, immersed in multiplicity—in externalization, reification, and fragmentation—the first *Shahādah* is a refuge that unifies the soul and draws it out of its inherent dispersion. It vicariously reestablishes the vision of man's true situation through impressing on the mind and heart that God is ultimately the sole reality, power, and help. The concrete sense of the presence of the first *Shahādah* in Muslim life is eloquently described in the following passage:

> To understand how decisive this formula is one must observe the place it occupies in the life of the ordinary Muslim, who will pronounce these words in every crisis and at every moment when the world threatens to overwhelm him, as he will when death approaches. A pious man, seized by rage, will appear suddenly to have been stopped in his tracks as he remembers the *Shahādah* and, as it were, withdraws, putting a great distance between himself and his turbulent emotions. A woman crying in childbirth will as suddenly fall silent, remembering; and a student, bowed anxiously over his desk in an examination hall, will raise his head and speak these words, and a barely audible sigh of relief passes through the whole assembly. This is the ultimate answer to all questions.[4]

Between Submission and Faith

Just as right thought is a necessary precondition for right activity, so the *Shahādah* is at once the first and most essential ritual activity as well as the necessary precondition for Islamic ritual engagement and religious life generally. The witnessing of the *Shahādah* both defines a given individual as a Muslim and binds that individual to the observance, in principle, of the other Islamic rites; the acceptance of both the reality of God and the guidance brought by the Prophet carries with it the inherent demand to draw out all of its implications for worship and servanthood. Through its acceptance, the *Shahādah* informs all the other Pillars of Islamic ritual practice—prayer, fasting, charity, and pilgrimage: without the underlying truths enunciated by the *Shahādah*, they would be meaningless and without purpose. In addition, the *Shahādah* serves as a decisive threshold that an indi-

[4] Charles Le Gai Eaton, *Islam and the Destiny of Man* (Albany: State University of New York Press, 1985), p. 55.

vidual crosses over, the function of which is to strengthen and confirm the will towards the new end that has been embraced by the soul.

The Islamic tradition distinguishes between the categories of right activity (*islām*) and right faith (*īmān*). Strictly speaking, to be a Muslim implies engaging in right activity, as embodied in the Pillars and more generally in the guidance of the Qur'ān and the Prophet; it does not strictly imply right faith. The Qur'ān speaks of this in the context of a particular incident:

> The Bedouins say, "We have faith." Say, "You do not have faith. Rather say, 'We have submitted,' for faith has not yet entered your hearts. If you obey God and His messenger, He will not diminish you anything of your works" (49:14).

The faith of an individual is intrinsically private, known only to himself and God; when a man once questioned the faith of another Muslim, the Prophet's sharp response was, "Did you open the heart and look?" The Pillars, embedded within the realm of human activity, do not directly engage the realm of faith, which is the realm of the heart itself. Yet, the very reason for the Pillars is to enable the heart to be purified so that faith may enter into it and be strengthened in it. The *Shahādah* itself lies within the domain of activity, corresponding to right speech or "the work of the tongue." At the same time, the *Shahādah* is directly concerned with the domain of faith and directly enunciates the essential content of faith. In this way, the *Shahādah* works to bind faith with activity at the very root of Islamic *praxis*.

Another means by which the "right activity" of the Pillars is coupled to "right faith" is through the *niyyah*, or formal statement of intentionality that precedes each rite. In pronouncing the *niyyah*, the Muslim states his intention to worship only for the sake of God and for no other end; in this way, the *niyyah* serves to both gather the attention and orient the heart. Every pillar is preceded by its appropriate *niyyah*, except for the *Shahādah* itself; the *Shahādah* incorporates the *niyyah* and is its own *niyyah*, and this is true of no other pillar. Just as the other pillars are meaningless without the truths embodied in the *Shahādah*, so the *niyyah* is impossible without the acceptance of the *Shahādah* and the essential truths that it bears. Just as the *Shahādah* incorporates the *niyyah*, so the *niyyah* implicitly bears the *Shahādah* within it, since it acknowledges both the reality and unicity of God as well as the guidance of God brought by the Prophet in the context of the specific rite that it addresses.

Thus, when a Muslim states his intention to "pray *salāt* for the sake of Allah and Allah alone," he implicitly bears witness to both the unity of God and the guidance of the Prophet, of which the *salāt*, or ritual prayer, is a part. Even when the *Shahādah* itself is not integrated into a given rite, as it is in the *salāt*, still, the *niyyah* serves as a kind of spoken echo of the silent presence of the *Shahādah* as it accompanies the rite. As indicated in the Qur'ānic passage above, the Islamic tradition often denotes right faith as a further level of human maturation beyond that of right activity or submission to God. Nevertheless, the fact that the *Shahādah* is the first pillar to be embraced and the one that defines a Muslim as such, while the *niyyah* is spoken prior to each rite, indicates that right faith, at least in a nascent sense, precedes right activity. Ultimately and practically, activity and faith cannot be truly separated, except conceptually; the *Shahādah*, in its close association of both, bears witness to this.

The Metaphysics of the *Shahādah*

The Qur'ān, in its language, is traditionally understood to be miraculous; the *Shahādah*, which may be taken as the quintessence of the Qur'ānic message, possesses, in its phrasing, a miraculous quality of its own, yielding an interpretive richness and depth that belies its brevity. From its few words, there spring a profusion of inherent meanings—to ask which of these meanings is "correct" is to miss the point; the *Shahādah*, like a faceted gem, may be viewed from a variety of perspectives, each of which displays a certain aspect of the whole, none of which is exhaustive. Since knowledge of God is an "ocean without shore," the *Shahādah* cannot be reduced to a flat, monolithic understanding: its very adequation to the task of bearing such essentialized knowledge—a task assigned by revelation itself—demands that it be open to the richness of the Divine Self-disclosure. Just as a religious tradition must possess the capability to address diverse human capacities and temperaments, so the *Shahādah*, in its inherent polyvalency of meaning, is able to address the whole of the diverse spectrum of human types and possibilities, for "We shall test no soul save to its capacity" (23:62).

Unity and Its Ramifications

As discussed above, the content of the first *Shahādah*—"no god but God"—is termed the doctrine of *tawḥīd*, or the unity of God. The word *tawḥīd* does not simply mean "one" or "unity" as does the related noun *wāḥid;* rather, *tawḥīd* is the verbal noun of the verb *wahhada* and signifies "asserting one," "declaring one," or "making one." To say that "there is no god but God" may be understood on several levels. Most immediately, *tawḥīd* signifies a straightforward assertion of monotheism and refutation of polytheism. In addition, other levels of meaning may be brought out by a consideration of what might constitute a "god." The Qur'ān addresses this issue with particular clarity in two passages: "And We [God] never sent a messenger before thee save that We revealed to him, saying, 'There is no god but I, so worship Me,'" (21:25) and "Have you seen him who has taken his own caprice to be his god?" (25:43). Here, a "god" is identified as what one worships, and such a "god" is not necessarily an external deity or idol, but may be something as internalized as one's own caprice. In this sense, even the committed atheist may "worship" and be in thrall to the "god" of nationalism, democracy, technology, or any of the other shibboleths that men give their souls to, not to mention the far more intimate "gods" of lust, wealth, and power. The statement of *tawḥīd* denies through the phrase "no god" the ultimate reality or claim of those "gods" that are social, psychological, or imaginary in character and asserts through the phrase "but God," the One God, who is ontologically real and holds true claim to the human heart.

Ultimately, the term "god" in the declaration of *tawḥīd* may be taken to apply to anything claiming independent existence or qualities. Just as the Prophet asserted that, "There is no power and no strength but in God," so the Qur'ān states, "O people, you are the dependent upon God, and God—He is the Independent, the Praiseworthy" (35:15). In short, everything in the cosmos, in so much as it is inherently perceived through the veil of multiplicity as self-existent and independent, is a "god" that is denied by *tawḥīd*, which asserts the vision of unity, of God as the source of all qualities and the sole Existent and Real. Thus, "there is no god but God" was modified by some members of the Islamic intellectual tradition to read "there is nothing existent but God" (*lā maujūda illā 'Llāh*). In this sense, the phrase "no god" (*lā ilāha*) indicates the annihilation of all phenomena as self-existent, while the phrase "but God" (*illā 'Llāh*) indicates the subsistence of all phenomena through God. As the Qur'ān reminds us, "Everything upon the earth is undergoing annihilation, but there subsists the Face of your Lord, Possessor of Majesty and Generous Giving" (55:26-27). God is the "Possessor of Majesty" in that, ultimately, He is the only Real; God is the "Possessor of Generous Giving" in that He bestows contingent reality upon the creation.[5] Far from denying the existence of the created world, the declaration of *tawḥīd* in the first *Shahādah* rather insists on acknowledging the world as created, as finding its ultimate ground in God.

We ourselves, as phenomena in the domain of multiplicity, are subject to the truth of *tawḥīd*. The surprising consequence of this situation is that we cannot affirm *tawḥīd* without embracing inherent contradiction, since the very act of affirmation implies the duality of subject and object. As the Sufi Ansārī of Herat pointedly remarks, "None has affirmed the Unity of the One, since all who affirm it deny it."[6] To say, "I bear witness that there is no god but God" (*ashhadu an lā ilāha illā 'Llāh*) is to arrogate to oneself the capacity to truly say "I"; but ultimately, God is the only "I," just as God is the sole Existent. As the Qur'ān states, "God bears witness that there is no god but He" (3:16). In other words, *tawḥīd* necessarily embraces both the objective and subjective poles of existence—both unity of being (*waḥdat al-wujūd*) and unity of witnessing (*waḥdat al-shuhūd*).[7] In this respect, the Islamic spiritual tradition refers to a realized sage not as a knower of God, but as a knower *by* or *through* God (*'ārif bi 'Llāh*). In a more mundane sense, the doctrine of the unity of witnessing asserts that all knowledge, all witnessing, is ultimately through God. As the Qur'ān states, "Vision grasps Him not, but He grasps vision" (16:104). The full statement of the first *Shahādah* in the testimony of faith binds these two perspectives together; the unity of witnessing is denoted in the phrase "I witness that" (*ashhadu an*), whereas the unity of being is denoted in the phrase "there is no god but God" (*lā ilāha illā 'Llāh*).

While the doctrines of unity of witnessing and unity of being address the fundamental subject-object polarity inherent in experience, they may also be viewed as specific examples of the general situation in which all manifested qualities find their root in God. Thus, "The Witness" (*ash-Shahīd*) and "The Real" (*al-Ḥaqq*)—corresponding to God as subject and God as object, respectively—are merely two of the many Divine names found in the Qur'ān that denote the manifested Divine qualities. The first *Shahādah* was often

[5] William C. Chittick, *Sufism: A Short Introduction* (Oxford: Oneworld, 2000), p. 36.

[6] Quoted in Sachiko Murata, *The Tao of Islam* (Albany: State University of New York Press, 1992), p. 49.

[7] For a fuller account of these interwoven themes, see Victor Danner, "*Shahādah*," *Parabola* 11:1 (1987).

reformulated by the Islamic intellectual tradition in terms of specific Divine qualities, such as mercy or power, resulting in such formulas as, "There is no mercy but the All-Merciful (*ar-Raḥmān*)," or "There is no power but the All-Powerful (*al-Qādir*)." In this way, the deep implications of meaning embedded in the first *Shahādah* were drawn out by the tradition far beyond the simple claim of monotheism, encompassing a profound understanding of God as the source and ground of all being, all knowledge, and all qualities.

Guidance and the Messenger

Just as the other Islamic rites are meaningless outside of the context of the truths embodied in the first and second *Shahādah*s, so the second *Shahādah* does not stand alone, but is predicated on the first *Shahādah*. Only when the truth of God as the sole divinity and real is established may the function of Divine guidance be addressed. Thus, when a Muslim witnesses to the truths of the two *Shahādah*s, the declaration of the first *Shahādah* necessarily precedes that of the second; this verbal ordering is reflective of the actual ontological ordering in which God precedes the Prophet, and in which reality precedes guidance. The form of the second *Shahādah*—"Muḥammad is the messenger of God" (*Muḥammadun rasūlu 'Llāh*)—points to this predication in the first *Shahādah* through its final word, "God." From God comes the function of guidance reflected in the word "messenger" (*rasūl*), and this guidance is particularized in the Islamic tradition in "Muḥammad." Thus, in its formulation, the second *Shahādah* reaches backwards from the absolute to the contingent, from the universal to the particular, from the eternal to the temporal—from the absolute reality of God (*Allāh*), to the universal function of messengership (*rasūl*), to the specific role of Muḥammad.

The declaration that "Muḥammad is the messenger of God" carries a number of distinct connotations. Most immediately, as mentioned above, the second *Shahādah* acknowledges the reality of Divine guidance for man, guidance that has been historically embodied—as taught in the Qur'ān and as evident in history—in the Divinely appointed messengers sent to different human communities.[8]

[8] The Islamic tradition makes use of two terms—"messenger" (*rasūl*) and "prophet" (*nabī*)—to refer to this function of embodied guidance. While there have been many prophets, sent to remind humanity and confirm guidance, there have been relatively fewer messengers, corresponding roughly to the founders of the world's great sapiential traditions. These messengers have necessarily also been prophets; that is, the role of messenger is established upon the preliminary role of prophet. Thus, Muḥammad is

The second *Shahādah*, then, identifies Muḥammad as a messenger appointed by God; the community to which he has been appointed is evident from context as the historical community of Islam.

Muḥammad, as messenger, is the bearer of guidance for his community most immediately through his being the recipient of the Qur'ānic guidance itself. In addition, he is recognized by the tradition as the embodiment, in his inner nature and lived example, of that guidance; as his wife 'Ā'ishah stated, "His character was the Qur'ān," while the Qur'ān asserts, "You have a beautiful example in the messenger of God for whosoever hopes for God and the Last Day, and remembers God often" (33:21). The Prophet, in his embodiment of the Qur'ānic guidance, is, for Muslims, the foremost exemplar of the normative human state, and for this reason, the emulation of the Prophet has always been close to the heart of Islamic piety and spirituality. The sayings (*ḥadīth*), activities, and manner of comportment of the Prophet, collectively referred to as his *Sunnah*, were meticulously recorded by the early Islamic community, serving as the basis by which a Muslim might participate in the Prophetic example—an example that encompasses Islamic ritual and devotional life generally.[9]

The Marriage of Wisdom and Method

Taken together, the two *Shahādahs* comprise an essential summary and resolution of our human situation. Immersed within the domain of multiplicity with its diverse qualitative possibilities, we often take the things of this world, including ourselves, as self-existent and ultimately real, while also tending to wander in the space of possibilities open to us. The first *Shahādah* reminds us that the reality of the world is fundamentally contingent upon God, the one and absolute reality;

understood to be both a messenger and a prophet. Properly speaking, his title should be "messenger" or "messenger of God" (*rasūlu 'Llāh*), as he was addressed by his companions; nevertheless, reference to Muḥammad as "the Prophet" has been long established in English usage.

[9] The *Sunnah* forms an establishing matrix for the sacralization of Muslim life, from greeting one's neighbors to eating at the table to buying and selling in the marketplace. The collected sayings of the Prophet, or *ḥadīth*, may be considered as part of the *Sunnah*; the *ḥadīth* forms the first and most important commentary on the Qur'ān and is an essential complement for unfolding its deeper meaning. Most significantly, the precise character of each pillar was not fully specified in the Qur'ān itself; rather, each rite was established in its detail through the example of the Prophet. That is, the Islamic rites themselves, while broadly indicated in the Qur'ān, are part of the *Sunnah* of the Prophet; in participating in the rites, one also necessarily participates in the Prophetic example. In this sense, a Muslim worships God, but worships through the Prophet.

the second *Shahādah* reminds us of those human possibilities that lead both to God and to human felicity. The first *Shahādah* is essentially static and ontological, whereas the second *Shahādah* is essentially dynamic and soteriological. The first *Shahādah*, in its claim to absoluteness and unicity, vertically pierces through the veil of multiplicity, whereas the second *Shahādah*, through its evocation of the Prophetic function, horizontally guides the soul within the very domain of multiplicity. The first *Shahādah* is like a lightning flash that illumines a dark plain; the second *Shahādah* is like a narrow road that is thereby made visible.

The two *Shahādahs* are at once an adequate essentialization of both a true metaphysics and an efficacious soteriology, and in this respect stand in direct contrast to modernity, which has rejected metaphysics and is insensate to soteriology. The entirety of the Islamic sciences may be viewed as the unfolding and adumbration of the implications of the two *Shahādahs*, in terms of the intellectual and realizational traditions and the juridical and ethical traditions, respectively. In this sense, the Islamic tradition may be seen metaphorically as a flowering tree that has grown from the two *Shahādahs*, which respectively contain, in seed-like form, the summation of those metaphysical truths and soteriological ways pertinent to the tradition.

The *Shahādah* at once confronts man and means to transform him; in their meeting, the partitioning of the *Shahādah* may be seen to providentially conform to the natural distinctions of the interiority of man, recognized traditionally as consisting of intelligence, will, and virtue. The first *Shahādah*, as the bearer of essential truth, informs man's intellect; the second *Shahādah*, as the bearer of essential guidance, informs man's will and virtue.[10] The ordering of the two *Shahādahs* reflects the primacy of the function of intellect in man,[11] while their conjoining corresponds to the wedding of doctrine and practice—of *orthodoxos* and *orthopraxis*—in "the marriage of wisdom and method."[12]

[10] Nasr, *Ideals and Realities of Islam*, pp. 134-135.

[11] On another level, the ordering of the two *Shahādahs* may also be understood in an ontological sense as reflecting the primacy of transcendence over immanence: thus, the Divine, while present in the world, can never be reduced to the world.

[12] To borrow an expression from Mahayana Buddhism.

Discrimination and Conformity

In respect of man's interiority, both *Shahādah*s deal with discrimination: the first *Shahādah* discriminates between the Real and the unreal; the second *Shahādah* discriminates between moral beauty and moral ugliness, between felicity and wretchedness. In this respect also, both *Shahādah*s deal with conformation: the discrimination of the intellect between the Real and the unreal *is* the conformity of the intellect to the Real; the "discrimination" of the will and virtue—if we may employ such an expression—makes possible the conformity of the will and virtue to beauty and felicity. In a sense, both *Shahādah*s address distinctions between greater or lesser existence: the first *Shahādah* addresses the absolute distinction between absolute existence and contingent existence, Unity and multiplicity; the second *Shahādah* addresses the relative distinction, within contingent existence, between guidance and misguidance, felicity and wretchedness, Mercy and Wrath. Just as the Divine Unity possesses a greater degree of reality than the multiplicity of creation, so, within the created order, Mercy possesses a greater degree of reality than Wrath; thus the *ḥadīth qudsī*, "My Mercy has precedence over my Wrath."

In respect of man's knowledge of God, the two *Shahādah*s may be seen as indicative of the fundamental conjoining of cataphatic and apophatic knowing—of saying and unsaying—inherent in the very nature of the Divine Self-disclosure. The first *Shahādah* may be interpreted as essentially an apophatic statement: all positive, knowable qualities are stripped from our conception (*lā ilāha*), and we are left with only a name (*Allāh*) signifying the Divinity as such. The second *Shahādah*, in contrast, may be seen as an entirely cataphatic statement: God (*Allāh*) speaks of Himself and delivers his recitation, his Qur'ān, to man, through the intermediary (*rasūl*) of the Prophet (*Muḥammad*).

Unity and Mercy, Transcendence and Immanence

The two *Shahādah*s may also be viewed from each of the two interrelated perspectives of transcendence and immanence.[13] Viewed with an eye towards transcendence, the first *Shahādah* denotes God as absolute and transcendent, while the second *Shahādah* denotes God's creative and merciful act in the manifestation of creation. Viewed with an eye towards immanence, the first *Shahādah* denotes God as at once transcendent *and* immanent, while the second *Shahādah*

[13] Frithjof Schuon, *Sufism: Veil and Quintessence* (Bloomington: World Wisdom, 1981), p. 162.

denotes God's guidance and mercy as operative in creation. Essentially, there is Unity and there is Mercy, and the conjoining of Unity/Mercy characterizes the fundamental nature of things; the two perspectives considered above place the demarcation between Unity and Mercy in slightly different locations, the first giving emphasis to ontology, in which the creative act itself is an essential act of mercy, the second giving emphasis to the human situation, in which mercy is viewed within creation; in this respect, the mention of Muḥammad in the second *Shahādah* may be understood to refer to both the Prophet and the function of revelation, as well as to the creation itself, of which Muḥammad is, in a sense, the plenary symbol.

Either demarcation between Unity and Mercy is necessarily indefinite: in reality, Unity and Mercy are bound up together and are subject to no such division, a fact that is reflected in the very binding together of the two *Shahādah*s. Put another way, to say absoluteness is to imply infinitude; the transcendent Unity by its very nature effulges into multiplicity and in that effulgence of creation, we find the essential Mercy of God. It is here that we find the mystery of the Hidden Treasure: "I was a Hidden Treasure and I loved to be known, so I created the creatures that I might be known."[14]

Another means of approaching the conjoined meaning of the two *Shahādah*s is through the traditional metaphor of existence as an image in a mirror,[15] in which the object reflected is real whereas the image, in comparison, is unreal; in this sense, "there is no god but God." However, the image, while possessing only an illusory and contingent reality, is nevertheless a true image of the object reflected; in this sense, "Muḥammad is the messenger of God." The first *Shahādah* denotes the provisional reality of the image; the second *Shahādah* denotes the perfection of the image as a symbol of the reality that it reflects. In this respect, according to a *ḥadīth*, "No one sees God who has not first seen His Prophet." The metaphysical understanding of created existence—suspended between relative unreality and symbolic transparency, between negation and perfection—is only complete when both *Shahādah*s are considered. The Qur'ān further clarifies this understanding in two key verses: "Everything upon the earth is undergoing annihilation, but there subsists the Face of your

[14] A well-known *ḥadīth qudsī*, or extra-Qur'ānic Divine saying.

[15] On the metaphor of existence as an image in a mirror, see William C. Chittick, *Imaginal Worlds: Ibn al-'Arabi and the Problem of Religious Diversity* (Albany: State University of New York Press, 1994), p. 25.

Lord" (55:26), which witnesses to the provisional reality of existence denoted by the first *Shahādah*; and "We shall show them our signs on the horizons and in themselves until it is clear to them that He is the Real" (41:53), which points to the symbolic perfection of existence denoted by the second *Shahādah*.

The Islamic intellectual tradition makes use of the terms *tanzīh* and *tashbīh*, respectively, to describe the incomparability or similarity of God with respect to creation. The first *Shahādah* is the decisive statement of *tanzīh*, of abstraction, distinction, and incomparability; the second *Shahādah* is the decisive statement of *tashbīh*, of analogy, integration, and similarity.[16] And yet to say *tanzīh* is also to say *tashbīh*, since the world is, and the perspective of God as incomparable demands as corollary that God be similar to the created existence of which He is the sole cause and source. Likewise, to say *tashbīh* is also to say *tanzīh*, since God is the Real, and the perspective of God as similar to contingent existence demands as corollary that He stand incomparably beyond it. Put more concisely, there is at once similarity *and* incomparability; there is neither absolute difference nor absolute identity. The unicity of God—*tawḥīd*—must necessarily be grasped as the integration of the perspectives of *tanzīh* and *tashbīh*, incomparability and similarity, transcendence and immanence.[17] The perspective of *tanzīh* is that of *exclusive* unicity; the perspective of *tashbīh* is that of *inclusive* unicity.[18] In this way, the two *Shahādahs*, as reflective of these two conjoined perspectives, are of necessity bound together as a concise yet comprehensive statement of *tawḥīd*.

The Mystery of He/Not He

The first *Shahādah*, taken in a more synthetic sense, may be seen to witness to both *tanzīh* and *tashbīh* through its partition into the *nafy*, or negation—corresponding to *lā ilāha* ("no god")—and the *ithbāt*, or confirmation—corresponding to *illā 'Llāh* ("but God").[19] The *nafy* asserts the transcendence and incomparability of God with respect to created existence, whereas the *ithbāt* asserts God's immanence and

[16] Here, see Frithjof Schuon, *Understanding Islam* (Bloomington: World Wisdom, 1994), p. 6.

[17] See Sachiko Murata & William C. Chittick, *The Vision of Islam* (New York: Paragon House, 1994), pp. 72-73.

[18] Here, see Schuon, *Sufism: Veil and Quintessence*, p. 134.

[19] The *ithbāt* may also be understood to refer to the *Allāh* alone.

similarity. Here, the field of *lā* and *illā*—of "no" and "if not"—to which the *Shahādah* is addressed is that of created existence: "no god" is present in creation because He is transcendent; "but God" is present in creation because He is immanent. This dual witnessing to transcendence and immanence is reflected in a phrase employed by Ibn 'Arabī—*huwa lā huwa*, He/not He.[20] The answer to whether the created order is real must of metaphysical necessity be "Yes and no," since it is at once God and other than God. Here, *lā ilāha* corresponds to *lā huwa* ("not He"), whereas *illā 'Llāh* corresponds to *huwa* ("He"). Viewed from a slightly different perspective, if the "Yes and no" is reexpressed as "No, but yes" we find the *ilāha* of the first *Shahādah*, balanced between the "no" of the *lā* and the "but yes" of the *illā 'Llāh*. In this sense, *ilāha*—"god"—may be understood positively as *huwa lā huwa* (or more precisely as *lā huwa huwa*—not He/He) which is the character of creation as such, suspended between the Divine and nonexistence. The one perspective places the locus of the simultaneity of He/not He in the entirety of the first *Shahādah*, whereas the other places it in the *ilāha*.

From the human perspective, the first *Shahādah* must of necessity begin with a negation (*nafy*) and proceed to an affirmation (*ithbāt*), given man's inherent false affirmation, or reification, with respect to the world: the negation counters this false affirmation and clears the ground for a true affirmation regarding the Real; as such, the negation necessarily precedes this second, true affirmation. From the perspective of ontology, however, there is no sequentiality with respect to negation and affirmation: rather, there is of necessity a simultaneous juxtaposition or superposition of both, since things are, in themselves, at once not God and God. The very nature of language imposes a sequential understanding of the first *Shahādah*, since the words must be taken in one at a time, rather than as a simultaneous whole; nevertheless, the very brevity of the *lā ilāha illā 'Llāh* may be seen as an approximation to simultaneity within the sequential bounds of language. One concomitant of this simultaneity of negation and affirmation is that the inverse of the evident understanding of the first *Shahādah* arrives at the same understanding: in the sense taken above, everything is not god (*lā ilāha*), since things possess no independent self-existence, but everything also is God (*illā 'Llāh*), since the Divine Being pervades all that is; taken inversely, everything is not god (*illā 'Llāh*), since only the Divine Being is self-existent, but everything also is God (*lā ilāha*), since the world is, but cannot be so by virtue of its own self-existence.

[20] William C. Chittick, *The Sufi Path of Knowledge: Ibn al-'Arabi's Metaphysics of Imagination* (Albany: State University of New York Press, 1989), p. 4.

Parallels between Illā *and* Rasūl

In one sense, the second *Shahādah*, which points to the manifestation of created existence from the Divine absolute, may be seen to be implicit in the *illā* ("if not") of the first *Shahādah*, which, as it were, opens the conditional possibility for this manifestation.[21] In another sense, the *illā* of the first *Shahādah* and the *rasūl* ("messenger") of the second *Shahādah* form a complementary pairing: the function of *illā* ascends from created existence upwards toward God; the function of *rasūl* descends from God downwards toward created existence. In this latter case, we must consider not only *rasūl* but also *risālah*, the message, which is not only the Qur'ān but also the cosmos itself, for the verses (*āyāt*) of the Book have their direct counterparts in the signs (*āyāt*) of the manifest world.

The *illā* of the first *Shahādah* is grammatically constructed from a conditional,[22] *in* ("if"), and a negation, *lā* ("not"), in which the conditional faces relative reality (*lā ilāha*) and the negation faces absolute Reality (*Allāh*).[23] The *illā* stands between the two realities and is a *barzakh*—an isthmus—that at once separates and conjoins them. Viewed from the side of absolute Reality, the negating *lā* of the *illā* denotes the ultimate unreality of created existence in the Face of the Absolute; viewed from the side of relative reality, the conditional *in* denotes the absolute Reality as prefiguring the conditional possibility of created existence. The *rasūl* of the second *Shahādah* evokes the two complementary relationships that stand at its heart: that of vicegerent (*khalīfah*) and servant (*'abd*). With respect to absolute Reality, the *rasūl* is the perfected servant and is, in a sense, effaced in the Face of the Absolute; with respect to creation, the *rasūl* is the perfected vicegerent and is the representative of the Absolute in creation. These two relationships—servanthood and vicegerency—are, as it were, the human ramifications of *tanzīh* and *tashbīh*, respectively;[24] in other words, the structure of the Prophetic function—which, in respect of servanthood and vicegerency, is that of man as such—is a reflection of the structure of the Real. Thus *lā* finds its parallel in *'abd*, and *in* finds its parallel in *khalīfah*; the *illā* is the *barzakh* between realities, the *rasūl* is the *pontifex* between them.

[21] On this point, see Schuon, *Understanding Islam*, p. 152.

[22] Termed an *istithna*, or "exception."

[23] Here, see Cyril Glassé, *The Concise Encyclopedia of Islam* (New York: HarperCollins, 1991), p. 360.

[24] Murata & Chittick, *The Vision of Islam*, p. 251.

illā ("if not") { *in* (if) / *lā* (not)

rasūl (messenger) { *khalīfah* (vicegerent) / *'abd* (servant)

contingent reality		contingent possibility		contingent negation		absolute Reality
lā ilāha	←	*in*	¦	*lā*	→	*Allāh*

illā: double-facing isthmus

plenary, positive contingency		contingent representation		contingent subjection		absolute Reality
Muḥammad	←	*khalīfah*	¦	*'abd*	→	*Allāh*

rasūl: double-facing pontifex

Parallels between Ilāha *and* Muḥammad

This consideration may also be extended to the *lā ilāha* of the first *Shahādah* and the *Muḥammad* of the second *Shahādah*. Here, *Muḥammad*—in reference to the Prophet, who is viewed traditionally as a "beautiful example" (33:21) and a "mercy for the worlds" (21:107)—may be understood as a plenary symbol of all that is positive in creation. In contrast, *lā ilāha* refers to the whole of creation, both positive and negative; the *lā* ("no") is absolute negation and the absence of God, whereas the *ilāha* ("god") is the symbolic reflection of the Divine in the created order. Here, *ilāha* may be reinterpreted positively, not as an independent and necessarily false divinity but rather as an adequate "sign of God," or *āyāt Allāh*.

ilāha (god): *either* {
- false self-subsistence / *human perspective*
- symbolic transparency / *Divine perspective*

Creation, understood traditionally as hierarchically stratified into degrees of reality, is bounded between these two limits, recognized respectively as the domains of Wrath and Mercy, of separation from and nearness to God. According to a *ḥadīth qudsī*, "My Mercy has precedence over My Wrath." This "precedence" bears ontological implications, in that that which falls under the domain of Mercy is more *real* than that which falls under the domain of Wrath; in this respect, evil and ugliness are privations not only of the good and the beautiful, but also of reality and of God. In this sense, *Muḥammad* finds its parallel in *ilāha*:[25] both pertain to the Divine Mercy, for Mercy (*Raḥmah*) is the nearest attribute to God. Muḥammad, as Prophet, clarifies both the domains of Mercy and Wrath for man while being himself necessitated by that very ontological Mercy that he demarcates in human terms.

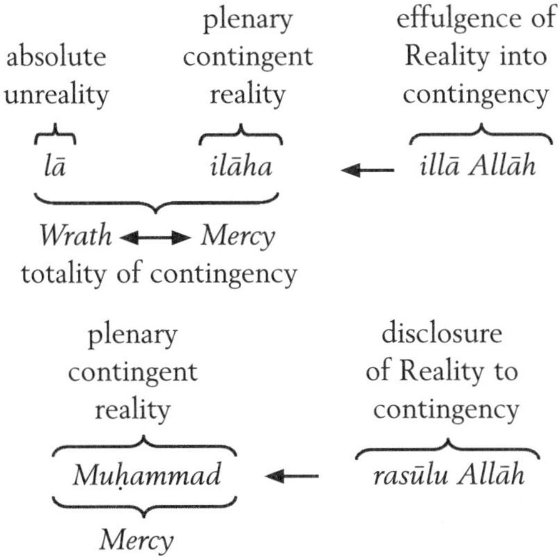

Just as Unity encompasses both transcendence and immanence, both absoluteness and infinitude, so Mercy is inherent both in the cosmogonic act—since existence is itself a mercy—as well as in the return to God. Mercy is like the breathing of Unity, the outbreath of infinitude giving existence to the creation, the inbreath of absoluteness drawing all things back to God. From the human perspective, the outbreath is the creation of man in the Divine form, while the inbreath is the Divine guidance given to man to assist his actualizing of the form, which is precisely the journey of return for man; put another way, with respect to man the outbreath is indeterminateness and possibility, the inbreath is integration and conformation. The con-

[25] Needless to say, this does *not* imply that Muḥammad is "a god": there is no divinization of the Prophet. Rather, *ilāha* may be reinterpreted positively, not as an independent and necessarily false divinity but rather as an adequate "sign of God," or *āyāt Allāh*.

joining of these two poles of Mercy is reflected in the *ḥadīth qudsī*, "If it were not for you [Muḥammad], I would not have created the worlds." Here, the full breath of Mercy is present, both the inbreath of Prophetic necessity and the outbreath of Divine creation.[26]

The first *Shahādah* may be seen to bear a double discrimination, one nested, as it were, within the other: it distinguishes not only between God as absolute Reality (*Allāh*) and created existence as relative unreality (*lā ilāha*), but also, within created existence, between that which is less relatively real (*lā*) and that which is more relatively real (*ilāha*). Each of the four elements of the first *Shahādah* may, in fact, be seen as a progression of ever-increasing reality, beginning with the absolute unreality of the *lā*, to the plenary contingent reality of the *ilāha*, to the effulgence into contingent reality of the *illā*, to the absolute Reality of the *Allāh*.[27] In a stronger sense, the relationship between the domain of Mercy and the domain of Wrath may be seen to precisely parallel, on a lower ontological level, the relationship between absolute Reality and relative or contingent reality. In this respect, the Qur'ān asserts, "I strike with my chastisement whom I will, but My mercy embraces all things" (7:156). Just as the Absolute precedes, encompasses, and dominates over the relative, so Mercy does so with respect to Wrath; once again, there is ultimately only Unity and Mercy—all else is contingent upon them.

The First Shahādah *and Human Possibilities*

The parallel between *Muḥammad* and *ilāha* bears specifically human ramifications, given the traditional understanding of the central state of man in creation. According to a *ḥadīth*, "God created Adam upon His own form (*sūrah*)"; the Qur'ān, expressing the same truth mythopoetically, affirms "He [God] taught Adam the names, all of them" (2:31). The specific task of man is to actualize that which he bears potentially, and in so doing become perfected as a vicegerent (*khalīfah*), as a representative—or representation—of God in the creation. The symbolic representation of the Divine form in creation is precisely the positive meaning of *ilāha* with respect to man, and it is this that Muḥammad, as the paradigm of human perfection, represents. The role of man is to transform himself—with the grace of God

[26] This description, while somewhat poetical, is reflected in Islamic metaphysics, where the same ontological reality is termed the "Breath of the All-Merciful" and the "Muḥammadan Reality." See Chittick, *The Sufi Path of Knowledge*, p. 139.

[27] See Schuon, *Sufism: Veil and Quintessence*, p. 134 for a slightly different interpretation.

and the example of the Prophet—from an admixture of *lā* and *ilāha*, of negation and plenary representation, into an *ilāha*, thereby fulfilling the form of his creation.

We have mentioned above that both *in* ("if") and *ilāha* ("god") may be interpreted as indicative of the function of vicegerency. Both, in fact, must be taken together if this function is to be properly understood: the *in* denotes the contingent possibility, with respect to God, of the Divine representation; the *ilāha* denotes the perfection of the represented form. Similarly, both the *lā* ("not") of the *illā* and *Allāh* must be taken together if the function of servanthood is to be properly understood: the *lā* denotes the negation or effacement of one's being and qualities; the *Allāh* denotes the Absolute, the source of all being and qualities, to which servanthood is oriented. The *lā* must be taken together with *Allāh* since servanthood is only conceivable with respect to Lordship; taken in its ultimate sense, in the mystery of the *lā 'Llāh* there is at once absence from self and presence with God.

There remains the initial *lā*, which stands alone as a singular negation: whereas both vicegerency and servanthood stand in relation to the Absolute, the initial *lā* is outside of such relation. This initial *lā* is placed in diametric opposition to the final *Allāh*, while also standing in contrast to the second *lā* of the *illa*; if *Allāh* indicates true Lordship and the second *lā* indicates true servanthood, then the initial *lā* might be said to indicate "false lordship." Both false lordship and true servanthood—indicated by *lā*—are negations, but the negation of the second *lā*, through its association with *Allāh*, is paradoxically full, while the negation of the first *lā* is simply empty. The negation of the initial *lā* stands maximally distant from the plenitude of the final *Allāh*, and is, in a sense, its inverse. This false lordship is at once an arrogation and reification of the self in respect of God, and is the natural concomitant of heedlessness and forgetfulness. It is the all too common human state, although certainly not the normative one; it could be said that the existential fact of the initial *lā* necessitates the revelation of the entirety of *lā ilāha illā 'Llāh.*

In the false lordship of the *lā*, the vicegerency of the *ilāha in*, and the servanthood of the *lā 'Llāh* we find in summary the entirety of human possibilities. Further, these are ordered by the first *Shahādah* with respect to rank and contingency: vicegerency is only possible through servanthood, which stands as the highest human possibility, whereas false lordship, the lowest possibility, is contingent upon the inherent function of vicegerency and is, in a sense, its radical misappropriation.

absolute unreality	symbolic perfection	contingent possibility	contingent negation	absolute Reality
lā	*ilāha*	*in*	*lā*	*Allāh*

false lordship — *khalīfah*: vicegerency — *'abd*: servanthood

human heedlessness — human perfection

The Interpenetration of the Two Shahādahs

The first *Shahādah* is most evidently a statement regarding the cosmos, just as the second *Shahādah* is most evidently a statement regarding paradigmatic man. Nevertheless, as the above considerations have demonstrated, the first *Shahādah* may also be understood from the perspective of man, just as the second *Shahādah* may be understood from the perspective of the cosmos, while both exhibit close parallelisms with respect to one another. This remarkable openness of the *Shahādah* to the intermixing of these two perspectives is reflected in the traditional understanding of the relationship between man and the cosmos, in which the cosmos, taken in its entirety, is the macrocosm ("great world") or "macroanthropos" ("great human being"), whereas man is the microcosm ("small world") or "microanthropos" ("small human being").[28] Both reflect the Divine form, the one in a dispersed and passive mode, and the other in a concentrated and active mode. This combination of parallelism and polarity marks the relationship between the cosmos and man, just as, in a general sense, it may also be said to mark the relationship between the two *Shahādah*s.

Similarly, although the first *Shahādah* primarily addresses metaphysics, while the second *Shahādah* primary addresses soteriology, viewed from another angle, both *Shahādah*s deal at once with both domains. Both *Shahādah*s, in their full testification, begin with *ashhadu an*—"I witness that"—while both end with *Allāh*; as such, both span the expanse between man and God. Taken from left to right,[29] the two *Shahādah*s denote the soteriological movement from man to God. Thus, in the first *Shahādah*, the saving act of the intellect is to negate the naïve conception of the world as opaque and self-subsistent (*lā ilāha*) and affirm the truth of the overwhelming reality of God in the Face of which the world is at once transparent and contingent (*illā*

[28] On the relation between the macrocosm/"macroanthropos" and microcosm/"microanthropos," see Chittick, *Imaginal Worlds*, p. 33.

[29] As read in English, Arabic being the reverse of this.

'Llāh); in the second *Shahādah*, the saving act of the will and virtue is to assimilate oneself to the Muḥammadan paradigm (*Muḥammad*) and in so doing, realize one's nature *in potentia* as both servant and vicegerent (*rasūl*) in respect of God (*Allāh*).

Human Perfection

negation of worldly reification		transparence of absolute Reality
lā ilāha	→	*illā Allāh*

perfection of intellect

conformation to Prophetic paradigm		realization of servanthood/ vicegerency
Muḥammad	→	*rasūlu Allāh*

perfection of will, virtue

Taken from right to left, the two *Shahādah*s denote the cosmogonic and revelatory movements, respectively, from God to man. Thus, in the first *Shahādah*, the creative act of God (*Allāh*), which, paradoxically, is necessary for the very comprehensiveness of His Unity, is the essential and eternally renewed cosmogonic act (*illā*) of creation (*ilāha*) from nothingness (*lā*); in the second *Shahādah*, the revelatory act of God (*Allāh*), which is necessary for the primacy of His Mercy, is through the function of message and messenger (*rasūl*), instantiated in the Prophet (*Muḥammad*).

Divine Self-Disclosure

nothing-ness		Divine creation		creative Act		absolute Reality
lā	←	*ilāha*	←	*illā*	←	*Allāh*

cosmogonic disclosure

Prophetic instantiation		Prophetic function		absolute Reality
Muḥammad	←	*rasūl*	←	*Allāh*

revelatory disclosure

This dual movement, from man to God as well as from God to man, recalls the *ḥadīth qudsī*, ". . . And if he takes one step towards Me, I take ten steps towards him. And if he comes to Me walking, I go towards him running."

The Methodic Use of the *Shahādah*

If the common human situation is one characterized by heedlessness (*ghafla*) and forgetfulness (*nisyān*), the Divine response is that of reminder (*dhikr*), a term that also refers to the Qur'ān itself. Central to the Qur'ānic message is the exhortation of man to *dhikr*—meaning remembrance, mention, and invocation. The intended human response to the Divine reminder is remembrance, and this remembrance is precisely the conformity of human thought, attention, and awareness to man's actual existential situation in the Face of God. The Qur'ān speaks of this in many verses: "O you who have faith! Remember God often, and glorify Him at dawn and in the evening" (33:41); "The remembrance of God is greatest" (29:45). As the above meanings of *dhikr* imply, this remembrance is effected through mention and invocation: as the Prophet said, "Let your tongue stay moist with the remembrance of God," while the Qur'ān, in several verses, exhorts man to "the mention of God's name" (*dhikr ism Allāh*).

The practice of invocation is central to Islamic spirituality,[30] as it is to that of every other sapiential tradition.[31] The foundational necessity for the practice of remembrance lies in the absolute and all-encompassing nature of the Divine Itself: as a Totality, God is ineffably absent but also totally present to us; this absoluteness and totality of presence demands as the necessary human response that man in turn become totally present to God; in this respect, the act of remembrance is, according to Ibn 'Arabī, precisely that of having "presence with the One Remembered,"[32] while Ibn 'Atā' Allāh

[30] As a general overview, see David Dakake, "The Practice of *Dhikr* in the Early Islamic Community" in Zailan Moris, ed., *Knowledge is Light: Essays in Honor of Seyyed Hossein Nasr* (Chicago: ABC International, 1999).

[31] In this regard, see Whitall N. Perry, *A Treasury of Traditional Wisdom* (New York: Simon & Schuster, 1971), pp.1001-42; see also the more introductory and approachable book, Gray Henry & Susannah Marriott, *Beads of Faith* (London: Carroll & Brown, 2002).

[32] Here, see William C. Chittick, "On the Cosmology of *Dhikr*" in James S. Cutsinger, ed., *Paths to the Heart: Sufism and the Christian East* (Bloomington: World Wisdom, 2002), p. 49.

defines it as "purification from heedlessness and forgetfulness by the constant presence of the heart with God."[33] The fundamental human necessity of remembrance implies a concomitant universality, one not only observed in other traditions, but also indicated by the Qur'ān itself, which refers to "cloisters, churches, synagogues, and mosques, wherein is mentioned the name of God" (22:40).

Ritual observance, such as formal prayer, draws man repeatedly out of the flow of the world, just as it draws his heart out of the flow of worldliness. But, as essential as such periodic observance is, its very punctuatedness prevents it from serving as a vehicle by which man may totally and continuously turn to God. The Qur'ān clarifies this well: "When the *salāt* [ritual prayer] is finished, scatter in the land and seek God's bounty, and remember God often" (62:10). In another verse, the Qur'ān clarifies the possibility of continuity of remembrance, speaking of those who "remember God standing, sitting, and lying on their sides" (3:191). The *dhikr* is the means by which the gap between the necessity of remembrance in principle and the actuality of ritual observance in practice may be drawn closed. Taken as a general term denoting the remembrance of God, one may speak of *dhikr* in *salāt*, just as one may also speak of the *salāt* as *dhikr*; more specifically, however, *dhikr* refers to invocation, to the repeated and, in principle, continual remembrance of God with the tongue and in the heart.

The Form of Remembrance

To remember God with the tongue requires a verbal declaration that is adequate to such a role, and it is here that the *Shahādah* plays what is perhaps its most vital function within Islamic *praxis*. The very qualities that exemplify the *Shahādah* as a summary creedal statement and occasional *viaticum* find their consummation in the invocation. Here, doctrine is combined with method, discrimination with concentration; both are refined in the systematic practice of *dhikr* and perfected in the awareness of the saints (*awliyā*). Here, the Absolute and relative are distinguished, and in that very distinguishing, the awareness and attention are conformed to the Real. As *viaticum*, the *Shahādah* is structured for invocation—it is a rope laid near at hand that man may cling to in his need, a talisman that he may carry always near to his breast. Islam flows forth from the Qur'ān, and in a sense, *is* the

[33] Quoted in Carl W. Ernst, *The Shambhala Guide to Sufism* (Boston: Shambhala, 1997), p. 92.

Qur'ān.[34] The Qur'ān, although a book, is first a recitation—for this is the very meaning of the Arabic word *qur'ān*—while its first revealed word was "Recite" (*'iqra*); the *Shahādah*, as the essentialization of the Qur'ān, naturally finds its expression in the essentialization of recitation which is invocation itself. In a sense, the nature of man demands that the *Shahādah* be accompanied by an associated method of integration and assimilation. Otherwise the *Shahādah* would predominantly address the intellect alone and fail to integrate the will and virtues. The extension of the *Shahādah* into the *dhikr* is precisely what enables the *Shahādah* to transform the entire being of man and not only the intellect.

While the second *Shahādah* may be applied in invocation in certain circumstances,[35] the most common form applied in invocation is the first *Shahādah* (*lā ilāha illā 'Llāh*) or its essentialization, the Divine Name (*Allāh*). While the second *Shahādah* is not typically verbally present in the invocation, it *is* operatively present in that the invocation is the epitome of the guidance brought by the Prophet, who called it "the best of all deeds, [and] the best act of piety in the eyes of your Lord." Here, the second *Shahādah*, the quintessential summary of salvific activity, is subsumed into the quintessential saving act itself. In this way, the invocation represents the fusion of doctrine and method, in which the two *Shahādah*s necessarily remain conjoined; the practice of the invocation is the congruent point where the two *Shahādah*s are bound together, where the way of the Prophet is *lā ilāha illā 'Llāh.*

Form and the Expression of Meaning

The Arabic sound form of the first *Shahādah* (*lā ilāha illā 'Llāh*), based upon the Arabic letters *alif*, *lām* and *hā'*, weaves the same basic units of sound through one another in a remarkable display of formal economy, symmetry, and harmony.[36] Just as the meaning of the first

[34] See Murata & Chittick, *The Vision of Islam*, p. x: "In a very deep sense, Islam is the Koran, and the Koran is Islam."

[35] See Martin Lings, *What is Sufism?* (London: Unwin Hyman, 1981), p. 76; in addition, it almost invariably plays a modified role in the extended litany (*wird*) recited in the various Sufi orders (*turuq*).

[36] In this respect, see Jean Canteins, "The Hidden Sciences in Islam" in Seyyed Hossein Nasr, ed., *Islamic Spirituality: Manifestations* (New York: Crossroad, 1991), p. 462. The formal expression of the first *Shahādah* might well be taken as a kind of minor proof for the sacred nature of the Arabic language. In the specific context of Qur'ānic

Shahādah affirms unity in the midst of apparent multiplicity, so the form of the first *Shahādah* parallels its meaning, being a kind of miniature in sound of the interpenetration of unity and multiplicity. The first *Shahādah* serves as a particularly adequate essentialization of the Qur'ānic message not only in doctrinal content but also in its form of expression, characterized by "a rhythm and assonance that capture in particularly condensed form the distinctive rhythmic and assonantal character of Qur'ānic language."[37]

The connection between meaning and form in the first *Shahādah* is also displayed in its written expression, where the vertical strokes of the *alif* and *lām* letters suggest the essentially transcendent meaning of the verse both by their vertical directedness as well as their vertical demarcation, which present, as it were, so many barriers between the absolute Reality of the *Allāh* and the relative reality of all in the verse apart from this. Similarly, the first *lā*, which orthographically resembles a scissors or blade, has often been compared poetically to a sword which "cuts off" or negates nonexistence,[38] thus reflecting both its grammatical and metaphysical meaning.

In a more profound sense, the first *Shahādah* may be understood as an expanded articulation of the Divine Name (*Allāh*) Itself.[39] Orthographically, the Name is made up of the four letters *alif*, *lām*, *lām*, and *hā'*;[40] so also, the first *Shahādah* consists of four words, each composed from the same three letters—*alif*, *lām*, *hā'*—from which the Name Itself is composed. Here, the doctrinal exteriorization of the meaning of *Allāh* which the first *Shahādah* represents, is reflected in its orthographic expansion from the Divine Name. Further, the Divine Name may be understood as carrying the first *Shahādah* within Itself:

Arabic, see also Gai Eaton, *Islam and the Destiny of Man*, pp. 73-76; also see Glassé, *The Concise Encyclopedia of Islam*, pp. 46-48.

[37] Michael A. Sells, *Early Islamic Mysticism* (Mahwah, NJ: Paulist Press, 1996), p. 46; see also Michael A. Sells, *Approaching the Qur'an: The Early Revelations* (Ashland, OR: White Cloud Press, 1999), pp. 146, 151.

[38] See Nasr, *Ideals and Realities of Islam*, p. 62; see also Annemarie Schimmel, "The Sufis and the *Shahādah*" in Richard G. Hovannisian et.al., ed., *Islam's Understanding of Itself* (Malibu, CA: Undena, 1983), p. 123.

[39] See Schuon, *Understanding Islam*, p. 151: "Now the *Shahādah* is nothing other than an exteriorization in doctrinal form of the Name *Allāh*."; see also Lings, *What is Sufism?*, p. 63.

[40] In this paragraph and the next, many of the points made closely follow the discussion in Canteins, "The Hidden Sciences in Islam", p. 460-463.

Allāh may be rendered grammatically as *al-ilāh* ("the God"), where *al* is a definite article ("the"); this definite article may be inverted to form *lā ilāh* ("no god"); thus, "the Name *Allāh*, the symbol of the Universal Being as much as it is an affirmation, contains in an implicit or subjacent manner the symbol of the absolute indetermination of Non-Being."[41]

The implicit embeddedness of the first *Shahādah* within the Name may also be seen in the distinction between the initial *alif* and final *hā'* of *Allāh*. Expressed orthographically, the *alif*—written as an extended vertical line—suggests the breadth and infinitude of created multiplicity, while the *hā'*—written as a small circle—suggests the concentratedness and absoluteness of transcendent unicity. Expressed vocally, the initial cry of the "a" leading to the extended exhalation of the "h" to the final ending in silence signifies the reabsorption of manifestation into its Principle; in this way, the very sound of *Allāh* is a verbal symbol of the return of man to God through his cleaving to the Name. This symbolic distinction within the form of *Allāh* may also be understood in the larger context of the first *Shahādah*. Here, the *alif* and *hā'* of the Name signify, respectively, the externalization of the Divine Essence and the Divine Essence in Itself: in the gatheredness of the *hā'*, God alone knows God; in the extension of the *alif*, God faces the creation—signified by the remainder of the verse—as Lord. Here, the final *hā'* of the Name has often been taken to signify *Huwa* ("He"), the Name of the Divine Essence[42] or Divine Self.[43] The *Allāh* may be said to signify the articulation of *hā'*—the Divine Essence—as it extends toward the created order, just as the *lā ilāha illā 'Llāh* signifies the articulation of *Allāh*—the Divine—into the creation itself.

A Darqāwī Shaykh, Muḥammad Bushārah, further expresses the manifold layers of meaning contained within the Name *Allāh*:

> The Name is made up of four letters which are read *Allāh*; if you remove the first letter those which remain are read *Lillāh* ("to God"); if you remove another letter—the first *lām*—what remains is read *Lahu* ("to Him"). Finally, there remains only the letter *Ha'*, which vocalized, is the Name "He" (*Huwa*: the Name of the Essence). In the same way, when we

[41] Ibid., p. 462.

[42] Lings, *What is Sufism?*, p. 85.

[43] Titus Burckhardt, *An Introduction to Sufi Doctrine* (Wellingborough, UK: Aquarian Press, 1976), p. 119.

> invoke the Name of God, its form gradually melts into the breath itself. The same happens to the dying man whose soul is resolved into breathing alone and leaves the body with the last breath.[44]

The Name, the Shahādah, *and Man*

Just as the first *Shahādah* is the summary of all metaphysical doctrine, so the Name is the synthesis of the entirety of the Self-designation of God with respect to man. The Name *Allāh* is understood by the tradition as the all-comprehensive Name (*al-ism al-jāmi'*), "since it alone designates God as He is in Himself in the widest possible sense, leaving out nothing whatsoever of His Reality."[45] Although God may be called by many names—of which the Qur'ān explicitly mentions ninety-nine—the Name *Allāh* is the "coincidence of opposites" (*jam' al-addād*),[46] what Ibn 'Arabī terms the "totality of the contrary names" (*majmū' al-asmā' al-mutaqābila*),[47] since it gathers together all the Names—with their mutual tensions and contrarieties—within itself. The very nature of the Divine Name as synthesis demands that the first *Shahādah*, as its doctrinal exteriorization, also be essentially synthetic in character.

As adequate expressions of the Real revealed to man, both the first *Shahādah* and the Divine Name are bound to a specifically human context. Given this, it is perhaps unsurprising that the interrelationship between the two finds a correlate interrelationship in man himself, where the verbal expression of the first *Shahādah* and the Divine Name correspond to the two fundamental human rhythms: the breath and the heartbeat. The *lā ilāha illā 'Llāh* is patterned to the rhythm of the breath, with the alternation between *lā ilāha* and *illā 'Llāh* corresponding to that between outbreath and inbreath; the *Allāh* is patterned to the rhythm of the heart, with the alternation between *al* and *Llāh* corresponding to the heart's contraction and expansion. Further, the ratio of syllables in the first *Shahādah* and the Name—7:2—conforms closely to the typical ratio of breath duration to heartbeat duration—again roughly 7:2, and itself the inverse of the ratio of breaths per minute to heartbeats per minute, falling in the

[44] Quoted in Glassé, *The Concise Encyclopedia of Islam*, p. 37.

[45] Chittick, *The Sufi Path of Knowledge*, p. 5.

[46] Ibid., p. 188; Chittick, *Imaginal Worlds*, p. 63.

[47] Ibid., p. 67.

approximate range (16-20):(60-80). In addition, the natural duration of the invocation of *lā ilāha illā 'Llāh* closely matches that of the breath, while the natural duration of the invocation of *Allāh* closely matches that of the heart, although it is also often drawn out in the practice of invocation to accompany the breath.

If the first *Shahādah* may be understood as being doctrinally unfolded from the Name, the practice of the invocation of the first *Shahādah* most often precedes that of the Name.[48] Thus, the Algerian Shaykh al-'Alawī guided his disciples in the following way:

> The *khalwah* is a cell in which I put the novice after he has sworn to me not to leave it for forty days if need be. In this oratory he must do nothing but repeat ceaselessly, day and night, the Divine Name (*Allāh*), drawing out at each invocation the syllable *ah* until he has no more breath left. Previously he must have recited the [first] *Shahādah* (*lā ilāha illā 'Llāh*) seventy five thousand times.[49]

This movement from the first *Shahādah* to the Divine Name in the practice of invocation in a sense parallels the movement from the invocation with the tongue (*dhikr al-lisān*) to the invocation with the heart (*dhikr al-qalb*);[50] the engagement of the mind with the doctrinal truth of the first *Shahādah* prefigures the engagement of the entire being with the presence of the Name.[51] This parallel is further sug-

[48] See Joseph E. Lumbard, "The Function of *Dhikrullah* in Sufi Psychology" in Zailan Moris, ed., *Knowledge is Light: Essays in Honor of Seyyed Hossein Nasr*, p. 266; See also Ibn 'Atā' Allāh al-Iskandari, *The Key to Salvation: A Sufi Manual of Invocation*, Mary Ann K. Danner-Fadae, trans. (Cambridge, UK: Islamic Texts Society, 1996), p. 89: ". . . and there are others who choose *lā ilāha illā 'Llāh* in the beginning, and in the end confine themselves to *Allāh*. These latter are the majority." A notable exception to this is Ibn 'Arabī, who began his practice with *Allāh* and moved later in his life to the invocation of *lā ilāha illā 'Llāh*; See Claude Addas, *Quest for the Red Sulphur: The Life of Ibn 'Arabī* (Cambridge, UK: Islamic Texts Society, 1993), pp. 50, 164-165.

[49] Martin Lings, *A Sufi Saint of the Twentieth Century* (Berkeley: University of California Press, 1971), p. 85.

[50] Without this thereby implying any rigid association between the *Shahādah* and the invocation with the tongue or between the Name and the invocation with the heart.

[51] See Seyyed Hossein Nasr, *Sufi Essays* (Albany: State University of New York Press, 1991), p. 50: "When Rumi writes in his *Mathnawi* that the adept must invoke in the spiritual retreat (*khalwah*) until his toes begin to say *Allāh*, he means precisely this final integration which includes the body as well as the mind and the soul."

gested in that the invocation with the tongue recalls the rhythm of the breath, corresponding to the first *Shahādah*, just as the invocation with the heart recalls the rhythm of the heart, corresponding to the Divine Name.

The invocation of the Name *Allāh* enacts the truth of *lā ilāha illā 'Llāh* with respect to the consciousness of the one who invokes (*dhākir*); the Name, when resonant in the heart of the *dhākir*, displaces all other thoughts. Subjectively, we "worship" our "gods" (*ilāha*)—and such "gods," particularly in the modern world, are legion[52]—through the attention and allegiance of our thought; to the extent that we give our thought to the Divine Name alone, we make *lā ilāha illā 'Llāh* true for ourselves. The purpose of *lā ilāha illā 'Llāh* is to carry the truth of *Allāh* as the Real to the domain of human awareness and consciousness so that the corollary truth of *Allāh* as the worshiped may be achieved; in this way, the *lā ilāha illā 'Llāh* forms a bridge between the objectively Real and our subjective commitment. In the words of Ibn 'Atā' Allāh, "No one says 'no god but God' correctly unless he negates everything other than God from his soul and heart."[53] Just as the second *Shahādah* is operatively present in the invocation of the first *Shahādah*, so both *Shahādah*s are operatively present in the invocation of *Allāh* in the heart of the *dhākir*.

The invocation of *Allāh* in the heart parallels, in a subjective mode, the nature of the Real Itself: ontologically, multiplicity is ultimately absorbed into the Unity of the Divine Essence; psychologically, the *dhikr al-qalb* absorbs the diverse thoughts into the Divine Name. Similarly, outside of the Divine Essence there is multiplicity in Unity, whereas outside of the *dhikr al-qalb* there are diverse thoughts underlain by the remembrance of God. In this respect, the Sufi Abū Sa'īd affirms, "The 'true saint' goes in and out amongst the people and eats

[52] See William C. Chittick, "The Role of Intelligence in Islamic Philosophy" (forthcoming): "This helps explain the modern-day 'polytheism' that is so obvious in numerous abstract notions that have been turned into pseudo-absolutes, thereby providing foundations for ideology. The names of our gods, after all, are legion—freedom, progress, democracy, nationalism, socialism, equality, science, development, capitalism."

[53] Ibn 'Atā' Allāh, *The Key to Salvation*, p.70; see also p.137: "Every man has one heart and one heart cannot be occupied with two things at the same time. When it is occupied with one of two things, it is excluded from the other thing, and this to the extent of its preoccupation with the first. Thus, it behooves the one who says *lā ilāha illā 'Llāh* that he intend by *lā ilāha* the expulsion of what is other-than-God from his heart. When the heart is empty of what is other-than-God, and when the authority of God is present therein, its light shines with a complete radiance, and His possession of it is perfect."

and sleeps with them and buys and sells in the market and marries and takes part in social intercourse, and never forgets God for a single moment."[54]

The Reality of the Name

The significance of the Name *Allāh* lies precisely in that it has been revealed by God as His Self-denotation to man. Although God has named Himself by many names, these are, in a sense, superseded and encompassed by the all-comprehensive Name *Allāh*. Both the Name *Allāh* and these other names are verbal denotations of ontological realities, just as the entire creation is described by the Qur'ān and understood by the Islamic intellectual tradition as God's Speech. The Divine names mentioned in the Qur'ān are the "names of the names" (*asmā' al-asmā'*); the names themselves are the ontological relationships between God and the created order. Ibn 'Arabī clarifies this matter:

> You should know that the divine names which we have are the names of the divine names. God named Himself by them in respect to the fact that He is the Speaker (*al-mutakallim*) [who reveals by means of His Speech].[55]

The relationship between the Divine names and the names of the Divine names finds its parallel in the relationship between the Divine Self-disclosures of creation and revelation. Just as both the cosmos and man are comprised of "signs" (*āyāt*), so also the Qur'ān itself is comprised of verses (*āyāt*) which are themselves signs; in the one are found the names (*asmā'*), in the other are found the names of the names (*asmā' al-asmā'*).

Just as the manifestation of the cosmos from the Divine Essence is only possible through the mediation of the Divine names—the manifold ontological relationships bridging Unity and multiplicity—so also God's knowledge of the cosmos is only possible through the names. As Ibn 'Arabī explains further:

> Were it not for the names, God would remember nothing, and nothing would remember God. So, God remembers only

[54] Mohammad Ebn-e Monavvar, *The Secrets of God's Mystical Oneness*, John O'Kane, trans. (Costa Mesa, CA: Mazda, 1992).

[55] Chittick, *The Sufi Path of Knowledge*, p. 34.

> through the names, and He is remembered and praised only through the names.[56]

Here, the *dhikr* is revealed as a twofold remembrance, at once God's remembrance of man through the Divine names, and man's remembrance of God through the names of the Divine names. As the Qur'ān states, "Remember me, and I will remember you" (2:152). It is man's speech, in the *dhikr*, which closes and sustains the circle of Being, for the Prophet has said, "The Hour will not come as long as there remains in the earth someone who is saying '*Allāh, Allāh.*'" The creation of man in the cosmos is through the Divine Speech in respect of him; the return of man to God is through man's speech—both on the tongue and in the heart—of the Name in respect of Him.

The essential relation between the ontological reality of a name and its verbal denotation in human language, as established by the Divine Self-disclosure in revelation, is what gives the names of the names—and in particular the Supreme Name (*al-ism al-a'zam*) *Allāh*—their inherent saving force, for they are, in Ibn 'Arabī's expression, "like robes upon the names":

Every name has two forms. One form is with us in our breaths and in the letters we combine. These are the names by which we call upon Him. They are the "names of the divine names" and are like robes upon the names. Through the forms of these names in our breaths we express the divine names. Then the divine names have another form within the Breath of the All-Merciful in respect of the fact that God is the Speaker (*al-qā'il*) and is described by speech (*al-kalām*).[57]

The Name *Allāh*, present in the invocation, bears a spiritual power (*walāyah*) by virtue of its all-comprehensive ontological root; in this respect, Ibn 'Atā' Allāh envisages the Name as the concrete embodiment of ultimate metaphysical reality.[58] The invocation of the Name, whether alone or as part of the invocation of the first *Shahādah*, brings this spiritual power to bear upon the consciousness of the *dhākir*. God, in addition to His inherent Mercy (*ar-Raḥmān*), possesses a specifically active mercy (*ar-Raḥīm*) that might also be termed compassion or grace. The invocation of the Name opens the

[56] Chittick, "On the Cosmology of *Dhikr*," p. 56.

[57] Chittick, *The Sufi Path of Knowledge*, p. 34.

[58] Ibn 'Atā' Allāh, *The Key to Salvation*, p. 17; see also Ibn 'Atā' Allāh al-Iskandari, *The Pure Goal Concerning Knowledge of the Unique Name*, Mokrane Guezzou, trans. (Louisville, KY: Fons Vitae, forthcoming).

dhākir to this mercy or grace through the conjoining of his consciousness—ultimately derived from the Divine Self-awareness—with the transforming power of the Name. It is not that the Divine mercy must be attracted, but rather that we must open ourselves to it; the Name, through the invocation, vehicles this grace to the *dhākir*. The Qur'ān clarifies this interplay between human invocation and Divine response: "When My servants question thee concerning Me—surely I am near. I respond to the call of the caller when he calls to Me" (2:186). Similarly, according to a *ḥadīth qudsī*, "I am with My servant whenever he remembers Me and his lips move [in mention of Me]."

Both the names and the names of the names are *barzakhs*—or isthmuses—between man and God: the names, through their ontological mediation between the Divine Essence and the creation, and the names of the names, through their dual verbal mediation, both in revelation and invocation, between the Divine and man. It is the Name *Allāh*—the name of the ontological name Allah, the all-comprehensive *barzakh* between the Divine and creation—which is at once the fulcrum and unifying element upon which the two *Shahādah*s are established. The presence of the Supreme Name *Allāh* sanctifies and vivifies the two *Shahādah*s through its inherent conjunction with the ontological reality which it robes; it is this conjunction that underlies the potentiality for human transformation through the methodic inculcation of the two *Shahādah*s in the practice of invocation. It is through the invocation of the Name in the heart that both *Shahādah*s find their consummation, not as verbal expressions, but as embodied operative truths present in the heart of the *dhākir*.

The Realization of the *Shahādah*

The first *Shahādah*, as discussed previously, is the declaration of *tawḥīd*, of Divine Unity, but *tawḥīd*—as a verbal grammatical form—implies the act of unifying, rather than simply Unity *per se*. To declare *tawḥīd*, then, is to unify and make one, but clearly this "making one" does not apply to God; rather, man must make himself "one." In this regard, the Sufi author Jāmī pointedly comments that "unification consists in unifying the heart."[59] There is a kind of homologous relationship between man and God in that the Unity of God as absolute and all-encompassing necessarily demands a unity and totality of response from man through worship, servanthood, and the unifica-

[59] Schimmel, "The Sufis and the *Shahādah*," p. 113.

tion of the heart. In this way, the declaration of *tawḥīd* reaches all the way from the ground of right activity (*islām*) in the witnessing of the first *Shahādah*, to right faith (*īmān*) in the conviction of the Unity of God, to the pinnacle of piety and spiritual excellence (*iḥsān*) in the unification of one's heart and the purification of one's intentions from all that is other than God. Put succinctly, God is a Unicity; man also must become unified if he is to be brought into proper relation to Him: for as the Qur'ān asserts, "Your Lord decreed that you should worship none but He" (17:23). The fundamental relation between Divine Unity and concomitant human unification is clarified in the most well-known Qur'ānic passage on *tawḥīd*, the short one hundred and twelfth chapter, titled at once *al-Tawḥīd* and *al-Ikhlās*, the latter meaning sincerity or purity—the attainment of *ikhlās* is precisely the unification of the heart (*tawḥīd*) in respect of the Divine Unity.[60]

Vision and Virtue

The perfection of man is to *live* the *Shahādah*, so that the words don't merely "stop at the throat," but rather are an expression of an overwhelming self-evidence of the actual nature of things and a continual awareness and alignment of one's being in accord with this nature:

> The *Shahādah* must be repeated and lived until the implicit realization has penetrated to the center of one's being, until through concentration upon the truth, and virtue, the individual substance is transformed and made itself adequate to the truth.[61]

It is here that the disproportion between mere verbal expression and accompanying inner transformation is found: the words of the *Shahādah* as spoken by an insincere man and a great saint are identical; their accompanying inner states, however, are completely different. On the face of it, the *Shahādah* is after all merely words—a collection of sounds accompanied by specific denotations of meaning. Yet on such words are civilizations built and souls saved—the received Qur'ān is also "merely" a collection of words, yet with the most profound impact both upon the historical stage and in the lives of count-

[60] See Qur'ān (112:1-4): "Say: 'He, God, is One; God—the Eternally Sufficient and Infinite Plenitude. He has neither begotten nor was begotten, and comparable to Him there is none.'" See also chapter 3, section "Unity and Uniqueness", pp. 28-31.

[61] Glassé, *The Concise Encyclopedia of Islam*, p. 360.

less individuals. The potential range of inculcation of the *Shahādah* is inherent in its very derivation, from the verb *shahida*, meaning both testification and perceiving: what the ordinary man testifies to, the saint perceives; what to the ordinary man is theory, to the saint is *theoria* or "vision."

Just as truth and way intersect in the practice of invocation, where the quintessential norm of the Prophet *is* the continual recollection of the absolute and all-pervading reality of God, so also in the profound realization of the *Shahādah*, there is a necessary fusion of knowing and being, vision and virtue. The realization of Unity is an integral knowledge, and as such, embraces the whole of man. Just as the two *Shahādahs* respectively inform man's intellect and his will and virtue, so they find their conjoined completion in the union of *'irfān* (or *ma'rifah*)—gnosis or illuminative knowledge—and *iḥsān*—moral beauty or virtue. The essential concordance between the two is established in the *ḥadīth* of Gabriel, where the Prophet spoke of *iḥsān* as to "worship God as if you see Him"; here, to "see God" is precisely *'irfān*. The saint strives to realize *lā ilāha illā 'Llāh* through perceiving the truth of *tawḥīd* and strives to live *Muḥammadun rasūlu 'Llāh* through following the Prophetic *Sunnah*, or norm; just as he embraces the vision of *lā ilāha illā 'Llāh*, so also he embodies the virtues of *Muḥammadun rasūlu 'Llāh*. In this sense, the *walī Allāh*—the "friend of God"—is at once sage and saint.

Degrees of the Soul

The Qur'ān, in speaking of human maturation in the return to God, makes reference to the *nafs*—the self or soul; it speaks particularly of three distinct stages in the development of the self: the "soul that enjoins to evil" (*al-nafs al-ammarāh bi-s-sū'*) (12:53), the "reproachful soul" (*al-nafs al-lawwāmah*) (75:2), and the "soul at peace" (*al-nafs al-mutma'innah*) (89:27). These three stages represent degrees of discrimination and conformation with respect to the Real, and as such, implicitly refer to the first and second *Shahādahs*, respectively. The "soul that enjoins to evil" has reified itself and is heedless of God, blown by the wind of its own passions and oblivious of the Prophetic norm; the "reproachful soul" has begun to see itself with objectivity and to recognize God as the Real, struggling against its tendencies toward corruption and dissipation; the "soul at peace" has turned fully from the unreal to the Real, having mastered its passions and cleaved to God. Here, the Qur'ān voices, "O soul at peace, return unto thy Lord, well-pleased, well-pleasing! Enter thou among My servants!

Enter thou My Paradise!" (89:27-30). The mutuality of "well-pleased, well-pleasing!" recalls the mutuality between those whom "He loves and who love Him" (5:59), a mutuality attained through the Prophetic example: "Say [O Muḥammad], 'If you love God, then follow me, and God will love you'" (3:31). The relation between the "soul at peace" and the inculcation of the two *Shahādahs* is further indicated in relation to the essential conjoining of the two *Shahādahs* in the *dhikr Allāh*: the Qur'ān speaks of "Those who have faith, their hearts being at peace in God's remembrance" (13:28); here, the same verb, *tama'nna*—to be at rest—is used to describe both the "soul at peace" and the heart of the *dhākir*.

The gradual maturation of the soul in its return to God is termed *tazkiyat an-nafs*,[62] where the verb *tazkiya* means at once purification and augmentation. *Tazkiya*, as purification, implies a necessary discrimination in one's being between the Real and the unreal, corresponding to the discrimination inherent in the first *Shahādah*; *tazkiya*, as augmentation, implies the assimilation of the Prophetic character and virtues, corresponding to the conformation inherent in the second *Shahādah*.

Idolatry and Struggle

This moral discrimination and conformation, as applied to the qualities of the *nafs*, must ultimately be applied to the *nafs* itself. In Islam, the greatest sin[63] is that of idolatry (*shirk*), of associating anything with God. The Islamic spiritual tradition has long recognized that the most subtle and stubborn form of idolatry is the idolatry of the *nafs*.[64] In this respect, the early Sufi Rābi'ah remarked, "Your own existence is a sin to which none can be compared."[65] This sin is the reification of the self, the ego, which thereby obscures the Divine Self at the heart of man; as al-Junayd enigmatically remarked, "Know that you are veiled from yourself by yourself."[66] This obscuring is suggested in the very

[62] An expression derived from the Qur'ān: see Qur'ān 91:7-10; see also Chittick, *Sufism: A Short Introduction*, pp. 40-41.

[63] See Qur'ān 4:116.

[64] For instance, see Ibn 'Ata' Illah & Kwaja Abdullah Ansari, *The Book of Wisdom & Intimate Conversations*, Victor Danner & Wheeler M. Thackston, trans. (Mahwah, NJ: Paulist Press, 1996), pp. 132-133, n. 18.

[65] Quoted in Lings, *A Sufi Saint of the Twentieth Century*, p. 125, n. 2.

[66] Quoted in Sells, *Early Islamic Mysticism*, p. 255.

meaning of the Arabic term for unbelief—*kufr*, to cover or to hide; here, the idolatry of the *nafs* is precisely the covering or hiding of God as the true Witness:

> The ego is at once a reflection of the Self which thus conveys an idea of what the Self is, but it is also its own impediment to union with the Self when, through delusion and pride, it refuses to admit its own provisional nature and give up its claims to self sufficiency.[67]

The first *Shahādah* may be understood as a direct rebuttal of human claims to idolatry, and as such, must also address the idolatry of the self. The struggle against the idolatry of the unregenerate self, the *nafs al-ammarāh bi-s-sū'*, is, in the words of the Prophet, the *jihād al-akbar*—the greater struggle or greater holy war—waged against the "greatest enemy"—"your self that is between your two sides." In this regard, the Prophet once said, in the context of the struggle against the Arabian pagans, that "I have been commanded to fight the disbelievers until they testify *lā ilāha illā 'Llāh, Muḥammadun rasūlu 'Llāh*." The weapons for the waging of the *jihād al-akbar* are precisely the two testifications of the *Shahādah*, as operatively applied in the practice of *dhikr*,[68] in this respect, al-Ghazālī teaches that the inner aspect of the one who performs *dhikr* must be exactly like that of one who is fighting for the single cause of God.[69] The greater struggle reaches its conclusion when the idolatry of the *nafs* is broken, when the self existentially testifies to the truth of *lā ilāha illā 'Llāh* and in so doing negates its own reification (*lā ilāha*), while affirming the Self as Real (*illā 'Llāh*); the self nevertheless continues to possess contingent reality, and as such, within its own contingency, conforms to the Muḥammadan norm (*Muḥammadun rasūlu 'Llāh*).

Annihilation and Subsistence

The idolatry of the self is, in a sense, the complement to the forgetfulness (*nisyān*) of God endemic to the human state; given this, it is

[67] Glassé, *The Concise Encyclopedia of Islam*, p. 414.

[68] See Seyyed Hossein Nasr, "The Spiritual Significance of *Jihād*," *Parabola* 7:4 (1983), p. 17; see also S. Abdullah Schleifer, "Undestanding *Jihād*: Definition and Methodology," *Islamic Quarterly* 27:3 (1983), p. 125.

[69] Abu Hamid Al-Ghazali, *Invocations and Supplications*, K. Nakamura, trans. (Cambridge, UK: Islamic Texts Society, 1990), p. xxiv.

perhaps unsurprising that, in the shattering of this most persistent of idols, it is the self that is forgotten in the face of the overwhelming presence of God. In the state of *fanā'*—annihilation or passing away from self—the ego consciousness falls away, dissolved into the Self-awareness of the Real:

> *Fanā'* is certainly a human experience. . . . But it is not solely a human experience. For when he does experience it, he is no longer himself. In this sense man is not the subject of experience. The subject is rather the metaphysical Reality itself.[70]

As al-Junayd summarily describes, "The *wujūd* [i.e. finding, existence] of the Real occurs through the loss of your self."[71] Similarly, Ibn 'Arabī remarks that the Prophetic phrase "if you see Him not," in the definition of *iḥsān* in the *ḥadīth* of Gabriel, may also be grammatically rendered, "if you are not, see Him."[72]

Correlate to the state of *fanā'* is the state of *baqā'*—subsistence in God. The first is, according to an early Sufi, "the annihilation of him who was not," while the second is "the subsistence of Him who has always been."[73] As the Qur'ān asserts, in a somewhat broader context, "The Real [*al-Ḥaqq*] has come and falsehood has vanished" (17:81). Expressed more fully:

> At the stage of *fanā'*, the pseudo-ego or the relative self has completely dissolved into nothingness. At the next stage [*baqā'*] man is resuscitated out of nothingness, completely transformed into an absolute Self. What is resuscitated is outwardly the same old man, but he is a man who has once transcended his own determination.[74]

[70] Toshikito Izutsu, *Creation and the Timeless Order of Things: Essays in Islamic Mystical Philosophy* (Ashland, OR: White Cloud Press, 1994), p. 13.

[71] Quoted in Sells, *Early Islamic Mysticism*, p. 131.

[72] Reza Shah-Kazemi, "The Metaphysics of Interfaith Dialogue: Sufi Perspectives on the Universality of the Quranic Message" in James S. Cutsinger, ed., *Paths to the Heart: Sufism and the Christian East* (Bloomington: World Wisdom, 2002), p. 149, n. 21.

[73] William C. Chittick, *The Self-Disclosure of God: Principles of Ibn al-'Arabi's Cosmology* (Albany: State University of New York Press, 1998), p. 84.

[74] Izutsu, *Creation and the Timeless Order of Things*, p. 14.

Ibn ʿArabī clarifies the relation between the two states when he remarks:

> Subsistence is your relationship with the Real . . . but annihilation is your relationship with the engendered universe. . . . None subsists in this path except him who is annihilated, and none is annihilated except him who subsists.[75]

The Qur'ān particularly points to the possibility of the experience of *fanā'* and *baqā'* in two verses: "And when they saw him, they so admired him that they cut their hands" (12:32), referring to the self-forgetfulness of a group of women when faced with the beauty of Joseph; and, "You did not throw when you threw, but God threw" (8:17), referring to the Divine "overshadowing" of the selfhood of the Prophet at the battle of Badr. However, the crucial verse elucidating the conjoined reality of *fanā'* and *baqā'* makes it clear that these are not solely subjective human states, but rather, the essential situation of all things: "Everything upon the earth is undergoing annihilation (*fanā'*), but there subsists (*baqā'*) the Face of your Lord" (55:26). The conjoined reality of *fanā'* and *baqā'* is precisely denoted by the first *Shahādah*, for the annihilation of the human self and the cosmos from their own claimed realities *is* the *lā ilāha*, while the subsistence of the human self and the cosmos through God *is* the *illā 'Llāh.*

If the struggle against the inherent idolatry of the self is, according to the Prophet, the *jihād al-akbar*, the consummation of this struggle is at once a victory and a martyrdom. The Prophet enjoined that one should "Die before you die": the one who dies in this struggle is a *shahīd*—both a martyr and a witness. He is a martyr, having become annihilated from himself; he is a witness, through the subsistence of the Divine Witness at the very root of his selfhood. In another *ḥadīth*, the Prophet said, "Man is asleep; when he dies, he awakes": although typically understood as a description of man's posthumous situation, in fact, it perfectly describes this prior, voluntary death, in which "sleep" denotes man's typical unregenerate state; "when he dies" signifies *fanā'*, and "he awakes" signifies *baqā'*.

For those who have passed through this martyrdom, the error of reification, both of the self and the world, has been expunged, and as the Qur'ān says of those who have died and been resurrected, their "sight today is piercing" (50:22); with that sight, they perceive the signs of God "on the horizons and in themselves" (41:53), and

[75] Quoted in Chittick, *Imaginal Worlds*, p. 61.

wheresoever they turn, whether outwardly or inwardly, "there is the Face of God" (2:115). Ultimately, in the full testification of the first *Shahādah* (*ashhadu an lā ilāha illā 'Llāh*)—this very word that means "witness"—the "I" that witnesses is the Divine "I," for "God bears witness that there is no god but He" (3:16), and "God suffices as a Witness" (48:28).

The Form of the Name

This profound experiential understanding of the ultimate identity between the selfhood of man and the Self-witnessing of God is, in itself, incomplete: it is true that, as the Prophet said, "He who knows himself knows his Lord," but it is also true that "The servant remains a servant and the Lord remains a Lord." While there is identity, there is also hierarchy, and the realization of the former in no way absolves the need for conformation within the latter. In a sense, the two *Shahādah*s may be understood in precisely these terms, the first giving voice to the truth of the essential identity between God and creation, the second giving voice to the demand for the conformation of man's being to the hierarchy of the Real through cleaving to the Prophetic norm. The essential mystery of the concurrence of identity and hierarchy is equivalent to that of unity and multiplicity: within unity, there is identity; within multiplicity, there is hierarchy—both are simultaneously present, both must be taken into account. The great themes of the Islamic tradition—Unity and Mercy—are simply reflective of this inherent nature of the Real.

Man, created upon the form of Allah, having been taught all the names, bears the potential to become perfected as the Divine Self-disclosure of the all-comprehensive name, Allah. Such a perfection requires that he bring the traces of the names latent within him into a state of maturation, fullness, and harmony. In this respect, the Prophet counseled, "Assume the character traits of God," or, as understood by Ibn 'Arabī, "Assume the traits of God's names."[76] Human moral traits and qualities are in fact the Self-disclosures of Divine attributes: thus faith, generosity, justice, patience, wisdom, love, and many other aspects of human character coincide with the Most Beautiful Names (*al-asmā' al-husnā*) of God. The names of God, the multiplicity of relationships bridging between the Divine Unity and created multiplicity, necessarily embrace hierarchy, for "My Mercy has precedence

[76] Chittick, *The Sufi Path of Knowledge*, p. 22; also ibid. p. 275.

over My Wrath."[77] Further, since they encompass multiplicity, they necessarily involve opposition and contrariety. In man, the names must be brought together (*jam'*) such that there is both an appropriate balance of opposites and a conformation to the hierarchy inherent in the Real. The fruit of this harmonious gathering of the names is their completed maturation in an integrated state of all-comprehensiveness (*jam'iyya*) coincident with the all-comprehensive name (*al-ism al-jāmi'*) Allah.

The completed maturation of human character traits in concordance with the all-comprehensiveness of the Divine name represents the perfection of human possibilities, what Ibn 'Arabī terms "perfect man" (*al-insān al-kāmil*). The possibility of this perfection is implicit in the second *Shahādah*, for, as the Prophet said, "I was sent [as a Prophet] to complete the beautiful character traits." More particularly, this possibility is inherent in the operative application of the first *Shahādah* in the invocation of the Name, for the Name is as the robe upon the ontological name Allah. Through the invocation of the name of the name one may come into conformity with the name; one becomes all-comprehensive (*al-kawn al-jāmi'*) through cleaving to the name of the all-comprehensive name (*al-ism al-jāmi'*), for all-comprehensiveness (*jam'iyya*) is the "fruit of meditation, concentration, and remembrance (*dhikr*)."[78] Through cleaving to the name of the name *Allāh*, man may become a perfected locus for the name Allah, and as such, may paradoxically embrace God in the entirety of His theophany, for, according to the *ḥadīth qudsī*, "My heavens and My earth embrace Me not, but the heart of My believing servant does embrace Me." Through the operative inculcation of the first *Shahādah* in the invocation of the Name, man conforms himself to the hierarchy of the names, and as such, places himself under Mercy, for Mercy is the highest and most intrinsic nature of the Real; as God attests, "*lā ilāha illā 'Llāh* is My fortress; whosoever enters My fortress is safe from My chastisement."

Here, in the consummation of man, in the realization of his essential identity with God and his conformation to the hierarchy of Being, we find also the consummation of Unity and Mercy, and as such the consummation of the two *Shahādahs*.

[77] See also ibid. p. 23.

[78] Chittick, *Imaginal Worlds*, p. 58.

Bibliography

ABD/DW ad-Darqawi, Mulay al-'Arabi, *The Darqawi Way*, trans. Aisha Bewley (Norwich, UK: Diwan Press, 1980).

ABR/NS Abil-Kheir, Shaikh Abu-Saeed, *Nobody, Son of Nobody*, trans. Vraje Abramian (Prescott, AZ: Hohm Press, 2001).

ADD/QR Addas, Claude, *Quest for the Red Sulphur: The Life of Ibn 'Arabi* (Cambridge, UK: Islamic Texts Society, 1993).

ADD/VN Addas, Claude, *Ibn 'Arabi: The Voyage of No Return* (Cambridge, UK: Islamic Texts Society, 2000).

ALG/GB Najm al-Din Razi, 'Abd Allah ibn Muhammad, *The Path of God's Bondsmen from Origin to Return*, trans. Hamid Algar (Delmar, NY: Caravan Books, 1982).

ALI/NB Ibn Abu-Talib, 'Ali, *Nahjul Balagha: Peak of Eloquence*, trans. Sayed Ali Reza (Elmhurst, NY: Tahrike Tarsile Qur'an, 1985).

ARB/MS Attar, Farid al-Din, *Muslim Saints and Mystics: Episodes from the Tadhkirat al-Auliya'*, trans. A.J. Arberry (London: Penguin, 1990).

ARB/SM Arberry, A.J. *A Sufi Martyr: The Apologia of 'Ain al-Qudat al-Hamadani* (London: George Allen and Unwin Ltd., 1969).

BAD/GS al-Haddad, Imam 'Abdallah Ibn Alawi, *Gifts for the Seeker*, trans. Mostafa al-Badawi (London: Quilliam Press, 1992).

BAD/LM al-Haddad, Imam 'Abdallah Ibn Alawi, *The Lives of Man*, trans. Mostafa al-Badawi (London: Quilliam Press, 1991).

BAD/MR al-Haddad, Imam 'Abdallah Ibn Alawi, *Two Treatises: Mutual Reminding, Good Manners*, trans. Mostafa al-Badawi (Chicago, IL: Starlatch Press, 2002).

BAL/NG Uftade, Mehmed Muhyiddin, *The Nightingale in the Garden of Love: The Poems of Uftade*, trans. Paul Ballanfat (Oxford, UK: Anqa Publishing, 2005).

BAY/PB Bayrak, Tosun, *Inspirations on the Path of Blame: Shaikh Badruddin of Simawna* (Putney, VT: Threshold Books, 1993).

BAY/PM Imam Birgivi, *The Path of Muhammad: A Book on Islamic Morals & Ethics*, trans. Tosun Bayrak (Bloomington, IN: World Wisdom, 2005).

BAY/SS al-Jilani, 'Abd al-Qadir, *The Secret of Secrets*, trans. Tosun Bayrak (Cambridge, UK: Islamic Texts Society, 1991).

BEN/SD Ibn al-'Arabi, Muhyiddin, *The Seven Days of the Heart: Prayers for the Nights and Days of the Week*, trans. Pablo Beneito & Stephen Hirtenstein (Oxford, UK: Anqa Publications, 2000).

BHA/DC Bhatnagar, R.S., *Dimensions of Classical Sufi Thought* (London: East-West Publications, 1984).

BUC/NL al-Ghazali, Abu Hamid, *The Niche of Lights*, trans. David Buchman (Provo, UT: Brigham Young University Press, 1998).

BUR/FC Burckhardt, Titus, *Fez: City of Islam* (Cambridge, UK: Islamic Texts Society, 1992).

BUR/LS ad-Darqawi, Mulay al-'Arabi, *Letters of a Sufi Master*, trans. Titus Burckhardt (Middlesex, UK: Perennial Books, 1987).

BUR/SD Burckhardt, Titus, *Introduction to Sufi Doctrine* (Bloomington, IN: World Wisdom, 2008).

CAD/TW al-'Alawi, Ahmad ibn Mustafa & Fatima Yashrutiyya, *Two Who Attained: Twentieth-Century Muslim Saints, Sayyida Fatima Al-Yashrutiyya and Shaykh Ahmad Al-Alawi*, trans. Leslie Cadavid (Louisville, KY: Fons Vitae, 2005).

CHI/DF 'Iraqi, Fakhr al-Din Ibrahim, *Divine Flashes*, trans. William C. Chittick & Peter Lamborn Wilson (Mahwah, NJ: Paulist Press,1982).

CHI/EG Sadra, Mulla, *The Elixir of the Gnostics*, trans. William C. Chittick (Provo, UT: Brigham Young University Press, 2003).

CHI/FP Chittick, William C., *Faith and Practice of Islam: Three Thirteenth-Century Sufi Texts* (Albany, NY: State University of New York Press, 1992).

CHI/HP Chittick, William C., *Ibn Arabi: Heir to the Prophets* (Oxford, UK: Oneworld, 2005).

CHI/IW Chittick, William C., *Imaginal Worlds: Ibn al-'Arabi and the Problem of Religious Diversity* (Albany, NY: State University of New York Press, 1994).

CHI/MR Chittick, William C., *Me & Rumi: The Autobiography of Shams-i Tabrizi* (Louisville, KY: Fons Vitae, 2004).

CHI/PI 'Ali ibn al-Husayn, Zayn al-'Abidin, *The Psalms of Islam*, trans. William C. Chittick (London: Muhammadi Trust, 1988).

CHI/PK Chittick, William C., *The Sufi Path of Knowledge: Ibn al-'Arabi's Metaphysics of Imagination* (Albany, NY: State University of New York Press, 1989).

CHI/PL Chittick, William C., *The Sufi Path of Love: The Spiritual Teachings of Rumi* (Albany, NY: State University of New York Press, 1984).

CHI/SD Chittick, William C., *The Self-Disclosure of God: Principles of Ibn al-'Arabi's Cosmology* (Albany, NY: State University of New York Press, 1998).

CHI/SS Chittick, William C., *Sufism: A Short Introduction* (Oxford, UK: Oneworld Publications, 2000).

CHO/AK 'Abd al-Kader, ibn Muhyiddin, *The Spiritual Writings of Amir Abd al-Kader*, trans. Michel Chodkiewicz (Albany, NY: State University of New York Press, 1995).

COR/AM Cornell, Vincent J., *The Way of Abu Madyan: Doctrinal and Poetic Works of Abu Madyan Shu'ayb Ibn al-Husayn al-Ansari* (Cambridge, UK: Islamic Texts Society, 1996).

DAN/BW al-Iskandari, Ibn 'Ata' Allah & Kwaja Abdullah Ansari, *The Book of Wisdom & Intimate Conversations*, trans. Victor Danner & W.M. Thackston (Mahwah, NJ: Paulist Press, 1978).

DAN/KS al-Iskandari, Ibn 'Ata' Allah, *The Key to Salvation: A Sufi Manual of Invocation*, trans. Mary Ann Koury Danner (Cambridge, UK: Islamic Texts Society, 1996).

DOU/TS Ibn al-Sabbagh, *The Mystical Teachings of Al-Shadhili: Including His Life, Prayers, Letters, and Followers*, trans. Elmer H. Douglas (Albany, NY: State University of New York Press, 1993).

ELI/DB Elias, Jamal J., *Death Before Dying: The Sufi Poems of Sultan Bahu* (Berkeley, CA: University of California Press, 1998).

ELI/TC Elias, Jamal J., *The Throne Carrier of God: The Life and Thought of 'Ala' Ad-Dawla As-Simnani* (Albany, NY: State University of New York Press, 1995).

ERN/SG Ernst, Carl W., *The Shambhala Guide to Sufism* (Boston, MA: Shambhala, 1997).

ERN/WE Ernst, Carl W., *Words of Ecstasy in Sufism* (Albany, NY: State University of New York Press, 1985).

FAD/ES Fadiman, James & Robert Frager, *Essential Sufism* (San Francisco: HarperSanFrancisco, 1997).

FER/QG Ferraro, Jennifer & Latif Bolat, *Quarreling with God: Mystic Rebel Poems of the Dervishes of Turkey* (Ashland, OR: White Cloud Press, 2007).

FID/LA Fideler, David & Sabrineh, *Love's Alchemy: Poems from the Sufi Tradition* (Novato, CA: New World Library, 2006).

FRI/SS Friedlander, Shems, *Submission: Sayings of the Prophet Muhammad* (New York: Harper Colophon, 1977).

HAR/LG Harvey, Andrew, *Love's Glory: Re-creations of Rumi* (Berkeley, CA: North Atlantic Books, 1996).

HAR/RS Qushayri, 'Abd al-Karim ibn Hawazin, *The Risalah: Principles of Sufism*, trans. Rabia Harris (Chicago, IL: Kazi Publications, 2002).

HAR/TR Harvey, Andrew, *Teachings of Rumi* (Boston, MA: Shambhala, 1999).

HEL/DS Helminski, Kabir & Refik Algan, *The Drop that Became the Sea: Lyric Poems of Yunus Emre* (Putney, VT: Threshold Books, 1989).

HEL/JR Helminski, Camille & Kabir Helminski, *Jewels of Remembrance: A Daybook of Spiritual Guidance* (Putney, VT: Threshold Books, 1996).

HEL/LS Helminski, Camille & Kabir Helminski, *Love Is a Stranger: Selected Lyric Poetry of Jelaluddin Rumi* (Putney, VT: Threshold Books, 1993).

HEL/RD Helminski, Camille & Kabir Helminski, *Rumi Daylight: A Daybook of Spiritual Guidance* (Putney, VT: Threshold Books, 1990).

HIR/DS Ibn al-'Arabi, Muhyiuddin, *Divine Sayings: 101 Hadith Qudsi*, trans. Stephen Hirtenstein & Martin Notcutt (Oxford, UK: Anqa Publications, 2004).

JAC/HL Maneri, Sharaf al-Din Ahmad ibn Yahya, *The Hundred Letters*, trans. Paul Jackson (Mahwah, NJ: Paulist Press, 1980).

JAC/QG Maneri, Sharaf al-Din Ahmad ibn Yahya, *In Quest of God: Maneri's Second Collection of 150 Letters*, trans. Paul Jackson (Louisville, KY: Fons Vitae, 2006).

JAM/UC Jamnia, Mohammad Ali and Mojdeh Bayat, *Under The Sufi's Cloak: Stories of Abu Sa'id and His Mystical Teachings* (Beltsville, MD: International Graphics, 2005).

JIL/BS al-Jilani, 'Abd al-Qadir, *The Book of the Secret of Secrets and the Manifestation of Lights*, trans. Muhtar Holland (Ft. Lauderdale, FL: Al-Baz Publishing, 1997).

JIL/RC al-Jilani, 'Abd al-Qadir, *The Removal of Cares*, trans. Muhtar Holland (Ft. Lauderdale, FL: Al-Baz Publishing, 1997).

JIL/SR al-Jilani, 'Abd al-Qadir, *The Sublime Revelation,* trans. Muhtar Holland (Ft. Lauderdale, FL: Al-Baz Publishing, 1993).

KAB/CI Kabbani, Muhammad Hisham, *Classical Islam and the Naqshbandi Sufi Tradition* (Fenton, MI: Islamic Supreme Council of America, 2004).

KAB/GB Kabbani, Muhammad Hisham, *Guidebook of Daily Practices and Devotions* (Fenton, MI: Islamic Supreme Council of America, 2004).

KAD/AJ Abdel-Kader, Ali Hassan, *The Life, Personality, and Writings of Al-Junayd* (London: Luzac, 1962).

KAZ/JR Shah-Kazemi, Reza, *Justice and Remembrance: Introducing the Spirituality of Imam 'Ali* (London: I.B. Tauris, 2006).

KAZ/OL Shah-Kazemi, Reza, *The Other in Light of the One: The Universality of the Qur'an and Interfaith Dialogue* (Cambridge, UK: Islamic Texts Society, 2006).

KHA/HP Khan, Inayat & Coleman Barks, *The Hand of Poetry: Five Mystic Poets of Persia* (New Lebanon, NY: Omega Publications, 1993).

LAW/MH Awliya, Nizam ad-Din, *Morals for the Heart*, trans. Bruce B. Lawrence (Mahwah, NJ: Paulist Press, 1992).

LED/SR Lederer, Florence, *The Secret Rose Garden of Sa'd ud-Din Mahmud Shabistari* (Lahore: Ashraf Press, 1969).

LEW/CP Lewisohn, Leonard, *Classical Persian Sufism: From Its Origins to Rumi* (New York: Khaniqahi-Nimatullahi Publications, 1994).

LEW/SS Rumi, Mevlana Jalal al-Din, *Rumi: Swallowing the Sun*, trans. Franklin D. Lewis (Oxford, UK: Oneworld, 2008).

LEW/WS Lewisohn, Leonard, *The Wisdom of Sufism* (Oxford, UK: Oneworld, 2001).

LIN/SP Lings, Martin, *Sufi Poems: A Mediaeval Anthology* (Cambridge, UK: Islamic Texts Society, 2004).

LIN/SS Lings, Martin, *A Sufi Saint of the Twentieth Century: Shaikh Ahmad al-'Alawi: His Spiritual Heritage and Legacy* (Berkeley, CA: University of California Press, 1971).

LIN/WS Lings, Martin, *What is Sufism?* (London: Unwin Hyman, 1981).

LOS/AM Losensky, Paul, *Farid ad-Din 'Attar's Memorial of God's Friends: Lives and Sayings of Sufis* (Mahwah, NJ: Paulist Press, 2009).

MAS/3P Massignon, Louis, *The Passion of Al-Hallaj: Mystic and Martyr of Islam, Vol. III* (Princeton, NJ: Princeton University Press, 1982).

MUN/KG al-'Alawi, Ahmad, *Knowledge of God*, trans. 'Abd al-Kabir al-Munawarra & 'Abd as-Sabur al-Ustadh (Norfolk, UK: Diwan, Press, 1981).

MUR/CG Murata, Sachiko, *Chinese Gleams of Sufi Light* (Albany, NY: State University of New York Press, 2000).

MUR/TI Murata, Sachiko, *The Tao of Islam: A Sourcebook on Gender Relationships in Islamic Thought* (Albany, NY: State University of New York Press, 1992).

NAK/IS al-Ghazali, Abu Hamid, *Invocations and Supplications*, trans. K. Nakamura (Cambridge, UK: Islamic Texts Society, 1990).

NAS/SE Nasr, Seyyed Hossein, *Sufi Essays* (Albany, NY: State University of New York Press, 1991).

NIC/IP Nicholson, Reynold A., *The Idea of Personality in Sufism* (Cambridge, UK: Cambridge University Press, 1964).

NIC/MI Nicholson, Reynold A., *The Mystics of Islam* (London: G. Bell & Sons, 1914).

NIC/RM al-Hujwiri, Ali, *Revelation of the Mystery*, trans. Reynold A. Nicholson (Westport, CT: Pir Press, 1999).

NUR/2T Nurbakhsh, Javad, *Traditions of the Prophet, Vol. 2* (New York: Khaniqahi-Nimatullahi Publications, 1983).

NUR/SF Nurbakhsh, Javad, *Sufism: Fear and Hope* (New York: Khaniqahi-Nimatullahi Publications, 1982).

NUR/SM Nurbakhsh, Javad, *Sufism: Meaning, Knowledge, and Unity* (New York: Khaniqahi-Nimatullahi Publications, 1981).

OKA/SG Ebn-e Monavvar, Mohammad, *The Secrets of God's Mystical Oneness or The Spiritual Stations of Shaikh Abu Sa'id*, trans. John O'Kane (Costa Mesa, CA: Mazda Publishers, 1992).

PEN/WG Sanai, Hakim, *The Walled Garden of Truth*, trans. D.L. Pendlebury (London: Octagon Press, 1974).

POU/KL Pourjavady, Nasrollah, *Kings of Love: The Poetry and History of the Ni'matullahi Sufi Order* (Tehran: Imperial Iranian Academy of Philosophy, 1978).

POU/SI al-Ghazali, Ahmad, *Sawanih: Inspirations from the World of Pure Spirits*, trans. Nasrollah Pourjavady (London: Keegan Paul Intl, 1986).

REN/KG Renard, John, *Knowledge of God in Classical Sufism: Foundations of Islamic Mystical Theology* (Mahwah, NJ: Paulist Press, 2004).

REN/LS Ibn 'Abbad, Muhammad ibn Ibrahim, *Letters on the Sufi Path*, trans. John Renard (Mahwah, NJ: Paulist Press, 1986).

REN/SD Renard, John, *Seven Doors to Islam: Spirituality and the Religious Life of Muslims* (Berkeley, CA: University of California Press, 1996).

ROB/SB al-Iskandari, Ibn 'Ata' Allah, *The Subtle Blessings in the Saintly Lives of Abu Al-'Abbas Al-Mursi and His Master Abu Al-Hasan Al-Shadhili: The Founders of the Shadhili Order*, trans. Nancy Roberts (Louisville, KY: Fons Vitae, 2005).

SCH/IW Schimmel, Annemarie, *I Am Wind, You Are Fire: The Life and Work of Rumi* (Boston, MA: Shambhala, 1992).

SCH/MD Schimmel, Annemarie, *Mystical Dimensions of Islam* (Chapel Hill, NC: University of North Carolina Press, 1975).

SCH/PS Qushayri, 'Abd al-Karim ibn Hawazin, *Principles of Sufism*, trans. B.R. Von Schlegell (Berkeley, CA: Mizan Press, 1992).

SCH/TC Schimmel, Annemarie, *A Two-Colored Brocade: The Imagery of Persian Poetry* (Chapel Hill, NC: University of North Carolina Press, 1992).

SCH/TV Schimmel, Annemarie, *As Through a Veil: Mystical Poetry in Islam* (New York: Columbia University Press, 1982).

SEL/EI Sells, Michael A., *Early Islamic Mysticism: Sufi, Quran, Miraj, Poetic, and Theological Writings* (Mahwah, NJ: Paulist Press, 1996).

SMI/PY Smith, Grace Martin, *The Poetry of Yunus Emre, A Turkish Sufi Poet* (Berkeley, CA: University of California Press, 1993).

SMI/RM Smith, Margaret, *Readings from the Mystics of Islam* (Westport, CT: Pir Press, 1994).

SMI/SE Smith, Margaret, *Studies in Early Mysticism in the Near and Middle East* (Oxford, UK: Oneworld Publications, 1995).

STA/GB Star, Jonathan & Sharam Shiva, *A Garden Beyond Paradise: The Mystical Poetry of Rumi* (New York: Bantam Books, 1992).

STA/RA Star, Jonathan, *Rumi: In the Arms of the Beloved* (New York: Tarcher/Putnam, 1997).

STE/SW Stepaniants, M.T., *Sufi Wisdom* (Albany, NY: State University of New York Press, 1994).

TAY/GW Ibn Taymiyya, *The Goodly Word* (Cambridge, UK: Islamic Texts Society, 2000).

THA/SU Rumi, Jalaluddin, *Signs of the Unseen: The Discourses of Jalaluddin Rumi*, trans. W.M. Thackston (Boston, MA: Shambhala, 1999).

UPT/DH Upton, Charles, *Doorkeeper of the Heart: Versions of Rabi'a* (Putney, VT: Threshold Books, 1994).

VAL/CD Valiuddin, Mir, *Contemplative Disciplines in Sufism* (London: East-West Publications, 1980).

VAL/QS Valiuddin, Mir, *The Quranic Sufism* (Delhi: Motilal Banarsidass, 1977).

VAU/TP Vaughan-Lee, Llewellyn (ed.), *Travelling the Path of Love* (Inverness, CA: The Golden Sufi Center, 1995).

VIT/RS Vitray-Meyerovitch, Eva de, *Rumi and Sufism* (Sausalito, CA: Post-Apollo Press, 1987).

WAT/IC Watt, William Montgomery, *Islamic Creeds: A Selection* (Edinburgh, UK: Edinburgh University Press, 1994).

WIL/DU Wilson, Peter Lamborn & Nasrollah Pourjavady, *The Drunken Universe: An Anthology of Persian Sufi Poetry* (Grand Rapids, MI: Phanes Press, 1987).

WIL/HW Kirmani, Awhad al-Din, *Heart's Witness: The Sufi Quatrains of Awhaduddin Kirmani*, trans. Peter Lamborn Wilson & Bernd Manuel Weischer (Tehran: Imperial Iranian Academy of Philosophy, 1978).

Index of Qur'ānic Verses

3:191 In the creation of the heavens and the earth, and in the alternation of night and day, there are signs for men of understanding; those who remember God while standing, sitting, and lying down, and reflect upon the creation of the heavens and the earth. 78, 83, 153

4:78 Say: "Everything is from God." 51

4:103 When you have performed the prayer, remember God standing, sitting, and reclining. 70

4:126 To God belongs all that is in the heavens and in the earth, and God encompasses everything. 34

4:142 The hypocrites seek to deceive God, but it is God who deceives them. When they stand up to pray they stand up lazily, showing off to the people and not remembering God save a little. 81

5:83 Whose hearts thrill with awe at the remembrance of God, or of those whose eyes overflow with tears when they hear what hath been revealed unto the Prophet. 83

5:109 You [God] are the Knower of the things unseen. 43

6:73 It is He who created the heavens and the earth in truth; and the day He says "Be!," and it is. 64, 125

6:74 He is the Knower of the Unseen and the visible; He is the All-wise, the All-aware. 43

6:103 Vision attains Him not, but He attains all vision; He is the All-subtle, the All-aware. 44, 125

7:55 Call upon your Lord in humility and in secret. 65

7:100 Did We will, We would smite them because of their sins, sealing their hearts so that they do not listen. 78

7:156 I strike with my chastisement whom I will, but My mercy embraces all things. 148

7:171 And when thy Lord took from the Children of Adam, from their loins, their seed, and made them testify touching themselves, "Am I not your Lord?" They said, "Yes, we testify"— lest you should say on the Day of Resurrection, "As for us, we were heedless of this." 105

7:205 And remember your Lord within yourself, in humility and awe, with subdued voice, at morning and evening. And do not be among the heedless. 70

8:2 Only those are believers whose hearts thrill with awe at the remembrance of God. 82

8:17 [O Muḥammad] you did not throw when you threw, but God threw. 41, 116, 168

33:35 Men and women who have surrendered, believing men and believing women, obedient men and obedient women, truthful men and truthful women, enduring men and enduring women, humble men and humble women, men and women who give in charity, men who fast and women who fast, men and women who guard their private parts, men and women who remember God abundantly—for them God has prepared forgiveness and a vast reward. 65, 67, 82

33:41 O you who believe! Remember God abundantly; and glorify Him morning and evening. 65, 152

35:8 He guides whom He will, and leads whom He will astray. 12

35:15 O men, you are the ones that have need of God; He is the All-sufficient, the All-laudable. 50, 136

38:65 Say [O Muḥammad]: "I am only a warner. There is not any god but God, the One, the Omnipotent, Lord of the heavens and earth, and of what is between them, the All-mighty, the All-forgiving. 29

39:22 Woe unto them whose hearts are hardened against the mention of God; those are in manifest error. 67

39:23 God has sent down the fairest discourse as a Book . . . whereat the skins of those who fear their Lord tremble, and then their skins and hearts soften to the remembrance of God. 79

40:7 Our Lord, You embrace every thing in mercy and knowledge. 43

40:60 Your Lord has said, "Call upon Me and I will answer you." 62, 63

41:6 Say [O Muḥammad]: "I am only a mortal, like you are. To me it has been revealed that your God is One God; so go straight with Him, and ask for His forgiveness. 29

41:38 Yet those who are with your Lord do glorify Him by night and day, and are never wearied. 70

41:53 We shall show them Our signs upon the horizons and in themselves until it is clear to them that He is the Real. 27, 33, 143

41:53 Suffices it not as to your Lord, that He is witness over everything? 43

41:54 Are they not in doubt touching the encounter with their Lord? Does He not encompass everything? 35

42:11 Nothing is like unto Him, and He is the Hearing and Seeing. 11, 12, 44, 122

43:36 And he who blinds himself to the remembrance of the All-merciful, to him We appoint an evil one for a comrade. 82

44:38-39 We did not create the heavens and the earth and all that is between

Index of Prophetic Sayings

Ḥadīth Qudsī

they seen it?" They reply: "No, O Lord, by God, they have not seen it." Then He asks: "And how would it be if they were to see it?" They reply: "They would be faster in their flight from it and greater in their fear of it." He says: "I call you all to witness that I have forgiven them." But one angel will say: "Among them is so-and-so who is not one of them, for he only came out of need." God will reply: "They are the sitting-companions. No-one who sits with them can be unhappy." 72-73

I was a Treasure but was not known, so I loved to be known; I created the creatures and made Myself known to them, so they came to know Me. 52, 142

My heavens and My earth embrace Me not, but the heart of My believing servant does embrace Me. 33, 170

My Mercy has precedence over my Wrath. 141, 147

My servant draws near to me by nothing dearer than that which I have established as a duty for him. And My servant does not cease to approach Me through supererogatory acts until I love him. And when I love him, I become his hearing with which he hears, his sight with which he sees, his hand with which he grasps, and his foot with which he walks. 122, 126

My true servant is the one who is in remembrance of Me when he faces his enemy. 80

O child of Adam, when you remember Me you are grateful to Me, and when you forget Me you are unfaithful to Me. 65

"There is no God but God" is My fortress, and whoever enters My fortress becomes secure from My chastisement. 15, 17

When I [God] love him, I am his hearing through which he hears, his eyesight through which he sees, his hand through which he holds, and his foot through which he walks. 55

Whoever says: "There is no god but God" and "God is greater," his Lord confirms his truthfulness and says: "There is no god but Me" and "I am the Great." And if he says: "There is no god but God alone," God says: "There is no god but Me alone." And if he says: "There is no god but God alone; He has no partner," God says: "There is no god but Me alone, and I have no partner." And if he says: "There is no god except God; His is the Kingdom and His the Praise," God says: "There is no god but Me; Mine is the Kingdom, and Mine the praise." And if he says: "There is no god but God, and there is no power nor strength save through God," God says: "There is no god but Me, and there is no power nor strength save through Me." 29

Ḥadīth

He who sits down without remembering God the Almighty has committed an omission which God will hold against him, and he who lies down without remembering God the Almighty has committed an omission which God will hold against him. 66

The Hour will not come as long as there remains in the earth someone who is saying "*Allāh, Allāh.*" 161

If a person's last words are "There is no god but God," he will enter Paradise. 17

If someone professes a hundred times every day, "There is no god but God, Who is alone; to Him belongs sovereignty and to Him belongs praise; He is powerful over everything," then he has as good as ransomed ten slaves, and a hundred good deeds are written down for him and a hundred evil deeds are erased from him, and this formula becomes a protection for him against Satan on that day, so that no one can bring a more meritorious deed than he did except by increasing the same act more than that. 18

If you are not, you will see Him, for He sees you. 104

If you let down a man with a rope to the lowest earth, he will fall upon God. 35

I have been commanded to fight men until they say: "There is no god but God." 8

I have been commanded to fight the disbelievers until they testify *lā ilāha illā 'Llāh, Muḥammadun rasūlu 'Llāh.* 166

I have brought nothing more important than the *Shahādah.* 132

I was sent [as a Prophet] to complete the beautiful character traits. 170

Let your tongue be moistened with the invocation of God morning and evening, and then no fault will fall upon you. 65

The likeness of him who remembers his Lord to him who does not remember his Lord is as the likeness of the living to the dead. 73

Make me into a light. 122

Man is asleep; when he dies, he awakes. 168

The Messenger of God has said: "When you pass the gardens of Paradise enjoy

The Prophet once asked his companions, "Shall I tell you about the best of all deeds, the best act of piety in the eyes of your Lord, which will elevate your status in the Hereafter, and carries more virtue than the spending of gold and silver in the service of God and meeting your enemy and slaying or being slain in the path of God?" They said, "Yes, O Messenger of God." He said, "The constant remembrance of God." 74

The Prophet said to Abū Hurayrah, "O Abū Hurayrah, verily every good deed you perform shall be weighed on the Day of Resurrection except the testimony that 'There is no god but God,' as it cannot be weighed in the balance. For were it to be put on the balance of him who has confessed that formula sincerely, then even the seven heavens, the seven earths and what is on them could not counterbalance on the scales the weight of the formula 'There is no god but God.'" 17-18

The Prophet said, "Renew your faith." "How can we renew our faith?" they asked. The Prophet replied, "Say always, *lā ilāha illā 'Llāh*." 18

The Prophet said, "The single-hearted are foremost." When asked, "O Messenger of God, who are the single-hearted?" he replied, "The men and women who remember God abundantly." 80

The Prophet was asked, "Which of the servants of God is best in rank before God on the Day of Resurrection?" He said, "The ones who remember Him much." I said, "O Messenger of God, what about the fighter in the way of God?" He answered, ". . . truly those who do *dhikr* are better than him in rank." 73

Reflect upon all things, but reflect not upon God's Essence. 44

Religion is sincere counsel. 69

Remembrance of God is firm knowledge of one's belief, immunity from hypocrisy, a fortress against Satan, and a guarded refuge from the Fire. 83

Show us things as they are. 109

The solitary ones take precedence, they who are utterly addicted to the remembrance of God. 83

There is no power and no strength but in God. 136

There is no power and no strength save in God, the All-high, the Tremendous. 41

Index of Sufi Authors

General Index

For a glossary of all key foreign words used in books published by World Wisdom, including metaphysical terms in English, consult: www.DictionaryofSpiritualTerms.org.
This on-line Dictionary of Spiritual Terms provides extensive definitions, examples, and related terms in other languages.

Biographical Notes

PETER SAMSEL is an independent scholar with wide-ranging interests in traditional metaphysics, symbolism, science, and art. He holds a doctorate in theoretical physics and is the author of articles and review essays in *Parabola*, *Sophia: The Journal of Traditional Studies*, and *Sacred Web: A Journal of Tradition and Modernity*. His article, "A Unity with Distinctions: Parallels in the Thought of Gregory Palamas and Ibn al-Arabi," which is singular in its detailed delineation of the profound parallels between Christian and Islamic mystical theologies, appears in the volume *Paths to the Heart: Sufism and the Christian East*, edited by James S. Cutsinger, which is part of World Wisdom's Perennial Philosophy series. An article on the Sufi metaphysics of Divine unity to be drawn from the Islamic testimony of faith, "The First Pillar of Islam," was selected by *Parabola* for their *Parabola in the Classroom* collection of scholarly articles for educators.

SEYYED HOSSEIN NASR is University Professor of Islamic Studies at The George Washington University. The author of over fifty books and five hundred articles, he is one of the world's most respected writers and speakers on Islam, its arts and sciences, and its traditional mystical path, Sufism. His publications include *Sufi Essays*, *Knowledge and the Sacred* (the 1981 Gifford Lectures), *Religion and the Order of Nature*, *Islamic Art and Spirituality*, *The Heart of Islam: Enduring Values for Humanity*, and *Islam: Religion, History, and Civilization*. A volume in the prestigious *Library of Living Philosophers* series has been dedicated to his thought. World Wisdom published *The Essential Seyyed Hossein Nasr*, edited by William C. Chittick, in 2007.

Other Titles in the Treasures of the World's Religions Series

The Essential Vedānta: A New Source Book of Advaita Vedānta,
edited by Eliot Deutsch and Rohit Dalvi, 2004

For God's Greater Glory: Gems of Jesuit Spirituality,
edited by Jean-Pierre Lafouge, 2006

The Golden Chain:
An Anthology of Pythagorean and Platonic Philosophy,
selected and edited by Algis Uždavinys, 2004

The Heart of Plotinus: The Essential Enneads,
edited by Algis Uždavinys, 2009

An Illustrated Introduction to Taoism:
The Wisdom of the Sages,
by Jean C. Cooper, 2010

In the Heart of the Desert:
The Spirituality of the Desert Fathers and Mothers,
by John Chryssavgis, 2003, 2008

Native Spirit: The Sun Dance Way,
by Thomas Yellowtail, 2007

Native Spirit and The Sun Dance Way,
as told by Thomas Yellowtail, documentary DVD,
directed by Jennifer Casey, 2007

Not of This World: A Treasury of Christian Mysticism,
compiled and edited by James S. Cutsinger, 2003

Pray Without Ceasing:
The Way of the Invocation in World Religions,
edited by Patrick Laude, 2006

The Shin Buddhist Classical Tradition:
A Reader in Pure Land Teaching, Vol. 1,
edited by Alfred Bloom, 2013

The Shin Buddhist Classical Tradition: A Reader in Pure Land Teaching, Vol. 2,
edited by Alfred Bloom, 2014

Zen Buddhism: A History, Vol. I: India and China,
by Heinrich Dumoulin, 2005

Zen Buddhism: A History, Vol. II: Japan,
by Heinrich Dumoulin, 2005

Other Titles on Islam by World Wisdom

Art of Islam, Language and Meaning: Commemorative Edition,
by Titus Burckhardt, 2009

Christianity/Islam: Perspectives on Esoteric Ecumenism,
by Frithjof Schuon, 2008

Emir Abd el-Kader: Hero and Saint of Islam,
by Ahmed Bouyerdene, 2013

Introduction to Sufi Doctrine,
by Titus Burckhardt, 2008

Introduction to Sufism: The Inner Path of Islam,
by Éric Geoffroy, 2010

Introduction to Traditional Islam, Illustrated: Foundations, Art, and Spirituality,
by Jean-Louis Michon, 2008

Islam, Fundamentalism, and the Betrayal of Tradition: Essays by Western Muslim Scholars,
edited by Joseph E.B. Lumbard, 2004

Maintaining the Sacred Center: The Bosnian City of Stolac,
by Rusmir Mahmutćehajić, 2011

Men of a Single Book: Fundamentalism in Islam, Christianity, and Modern Thought,
by Mateus Soares de Azevedo, 2010

The Mystics of Islam,
by Reynold A. Nicholson, 2002

Outline of Sufism: The Essentials of Islamic Spirituality,
by William Stoddart, 2012

The Path of Muhammad: A Book on Islamic Morals and Ethics by Imam Birgivi,
interpreted by Shaykh Tosun Bayrak, 2005

Paths to the Heart: Sufism and the Christian East,
edited by James S. Cutsinger, 2003

Paths to Transcendence: According to Shankara, Ibn Arabi, and Meister Eckhart,
by Reza Shah-Kazemi, 2006

The Sacred Foundations of Justice in Islam: The Teachings of 'Ali ibn Abi Talib,
edited by M. Ali Lakhani, 2006

A Spirit of Tolerance: The Inspiring Life of Tierno Bokar,
by Amadou Hampaté Bâ, 2008

The Sufi Doctrine of Rumi: Illustrated Edition
by William C. Chittick, 2005

Sufism: Love and Wisdom,
edited by Jean-Louis Michon and Roger Gaetani, 2006

Sufism: Veil and Quintessence,
by Frithjof Schuon, 2007

Understanding Islam,
by Frithjof Schuon, 2011

Universal Dimensions of Islam: Studies in Comparative Religion,
edited by Patrick Laude, 2010

The Universal Spirit of Islam: From the Koran and Hadith,
edited by Judith and Michael Oren Fitzgerald, 2006

Unveiling the Garden of Love: Mystical Symbolism in Layla Majnun and Gita Govinda,
by Lalita Sinha, 2008

What Does Islam Mean in Today's World: Religion, Politics, Spirituality,
by William Stoddart, 2012

Wisdom's Journey: Living the Spirit of Islam in the Modern World,
by John Herlihy, 2009